PUBLIC RECORD OFFICE READERS' GUIDE NO 9

MAPS FOR
FAMILY HISTORY

A Guide to the records of the Tithe, Valuation Office, and National Farm Surveys of England and Wales, 1836 - 1943

by

William Foot

PRO Publications

PRO Publications
Chancery Lane
London
WC2A 1LR
© Crown Copyright 1994
ISBN 1 873162 17 0

A catalogue card for this book is available from the British Library

CONTENTS

ILLUSTRATIONS

GENERAL INFORMATION

At present the PRO is divided between two buildings. The records described in this **Reader's Guide** are housed at Kew. If you are in doubt about which to visit for other records, telephone 081-876-3444.

Public Record Office, Ruskin Avenue, Kew, Surrey TW9 4DU
Tel: 081-876-3444
Opening hours: 9.30 to 5.00pm Monday to Friday. You do not need to make an appointment.
Closed on public holidays and for annual stocktaking (usually the first two weeks in October).
Shop open 9.30am to 4.45pm.

Public Record Office, Chancery Lane, London WC2A 1LR
Tel: 081-876-3444
Opening hours: 9.30am to 5.00pm Monday to Friday; the Census Rooms are also open from 9.30am to 5.00pm on Saturdays.
You do not need to make an appointment.
Closed on public holidays and for annual stocktaking (usually the first two weeks in October).
Museum and shop open 9.30am to 4.45pm.

In 1996 the Chancery Lane building will close and all records will be housed at Kew. Contact the NewPRO team on the above number extension 2524 for details.

When you first visit the PRO, bring with you a formal document (eg: driving licence or cheque card) bearing your name and signature. If you are not a British citizen you will need to bring your passport or national identity card. You can then be issued, free of charge, with a Reader's Ticket. Without a Ticket you cannot be admitted to the Reading Rooms or order documents. You do not need one to visit the Census Room or the Museum at Chancery Lane.
You may only use pencils in the reading rooms. Pens of any kind are not allowed. You may use personal computers, typewriters and tape recorders in most of the reading rooms. For a full list of general and reading room rules, please ask for General Information Leaflet no 27: *Rules for Readers*.

PREFACE

The Public Record Office (referred to throughout this book as the PRO) is rich in its holdings of maps. A conservative estimate puts the number in its custody as six million, of which only an approximate one million have been catalogued, listed, or otherwise separately identified.

Maps can form discrete document classes, eg First World War Trench Maps (WO 297), Bomb Census Maps (HO 193), Colonial Office Maps and Plans (CO 700), Ordnance Survey Boundary Record Sheets (OS 41), or Maps and Plans of Ancient Monuments and Historic Buildings (WORK 31), to name just a few such classes. The great majority, however, are contained simply within the documents - the reports, despatches, files, and other papers - to which they relate, and may be totally unrecorded. The PRO has an on-going programme of work to identify as many such maps as possible, and add them to a database from which summary catalogues can be generated. Some 35,000 maps have so far been recorded in this manner. However, where a map is vulnerable to loss or damage, it is the PRO's policy to extract the map from its parent document and to preserve it separately with a full archival catalogue description. Naturally, in such cases, the record of the map's provenance is securely maintained. Despite the best efforts of the PRO's small map team, some five million maps remain to be discovered, and the services of readers[1] are called upon to help find as many of these as possible!

If you are using a document, and find a map within, please let staff have a note of it (there is a form available for this purpose). If the map has already been recorded, the front of the document will be stamped, 'Maps Recorded'. Such assistance from readers is of the greatest value.

Genealogists form the PRO's largest user group. Each day brings enquiries to the Kew Office for military service records, for merchant seamen's services, for records of apprentices, ships' passenger lists, railway staff records, records of RAF aircrew, and so on. At present, quite low down on the family historian's list of priorities, are the maps of which the PRO's holdings are so full. But the demand in recent years for maps as an aid to family history research has grown rapidly, largely due to the three particular groups of maps (and their associated records) which form the principal subject of this book.

---

[1] 'Readers' is the term used by the PRO for members of the public visiting in person to make use of the records.

Until four years ago, the maps most asked for in the Map Room[1] (by all categories of record users) were the Tithe Maps. This demand has now been well overtaken by the considerable public use of the Valuation Office records, and in the course of the last three years, since the records became open for public inspection, interest in the National Farm Survey has grown steadily as well. This guide aims to stimulate further readers' knowledge and use of these records.

This book could not have been written without drawing upon the knowledge of colleagues whose expertise with these records is developed from years of experience of answering readers' enquiries. My particular thanks are to Geraldine Beech and Garth Thomas of the Map Department for their time and patience in answering my questions and in suggesting new sources of information to me. I would also like to thank Dr B M Short of the University of Sussex and Dr P S Barnwell of the Royal Commission on the Historical Monuments of England, to whom I am much indebted for their scholarship which illuminates many aspects of these record sources.

[1]For information on the Map Room at Kew please ask for General Information Leaflet No. 91: *Maps in the Public Record Office*

1. THE USE OF MAPS FOR FAMILY HISTORY

The main usage of maps by family historians can be set out conveniently as follows:-

(a) Maps to show where a place-name connected with a family history is situated.

A genealogist on discovering, for example, that an ancestor was born in Trottiscliffe in Kent will very likely want to find that place, not only on a modern map, but on a map contemporary with the date of birth.

The PRO has excellent published and documentary resources to answer such enquiries. In addition to atlases and gazetteers on open shelves in the Map Room at Kew, there are copies of many of the fine mid to late eighteenth-century county surveys included in the class of War Office Maps (WO 78). The Tithe Maps (IR 30) (see Chapter 3) provide the first large-scale mapping of many parishes of the country. In the Map Room also are bound sets of the first edition of the 1 inch Ordnance Survey, a further set of 1 inch Ordnance Survey sheets of c. 1890, 6 inch Ordnance Survey sheets of about the same date for a number of counties, and copies of Rocque's Plan of London & Westminster (1746) and that of Bowles (1801), both with street indexes. Reference should also be made to the published catalogue, *Maps and Plans in the Public Record Office: Vol. 1 British Isles* (1967), and to the catalogue cards in the Map Room. Consult as well PRO General Information Leaflet 4 *The Map Room Kew* and PRO Records Information Leaflet 91 *Maps in the Public Record Office* (these leaflets are available at both Chancery Lane and Kew).

For places overseas, the map resources described in Records Information Leaflet 91 should be utilized, together with atlases and gazetteers available in the Map Room. The PRO has many land grant maps, or plats, (for example, in the records of the East Florida Claims Commission (T 77), but also for many other territories of the former British Empire) which actually record the landowner's name on the map that shows his landholding. The published catalogues, *Maps and Plans in the Public Record Office: Vol. 2 America and West Indies* (1974) and *Vol. 3 Africa* (1982) will be useful to locate such maps.

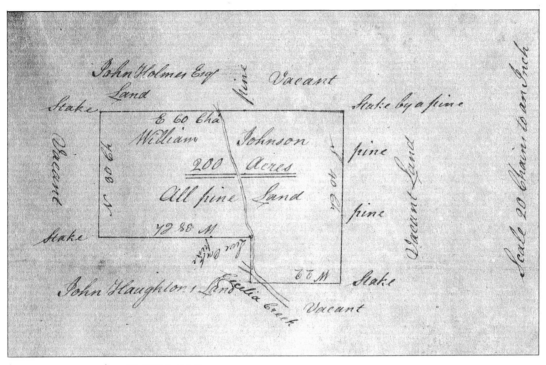

ILLUSTRATION 1   **T 77/12, f 97**
Plat showing land in East Florida granted to William Johnson in 1772. At the edge of the plat, the
names of the adjoining landowners, John Holmes and John Haughton, are given.

(b) Maps to increase substantially knowledge of places, buildings, and events connected with an individual's life.

For example, a reader who is using British Army Unit War Diaries for the First
World War (WO 95) to trace the places where a forebear served can gain a greatly
enhanced knowledge of that service by referring to the class of Trench Maps
(WO 297). These will show, for example, the grim detail of the opposing trench
systems and their lines of communication, as well as the place-names referred to in
the war diary.

Similarly, the PRO is rich in maps illustrating other military and naval operations,
and in maps and plans of buildings that an ancestor might have known, eg coastguard stations, RAF bases, workhouses, schools, railway stations and government
buildings.

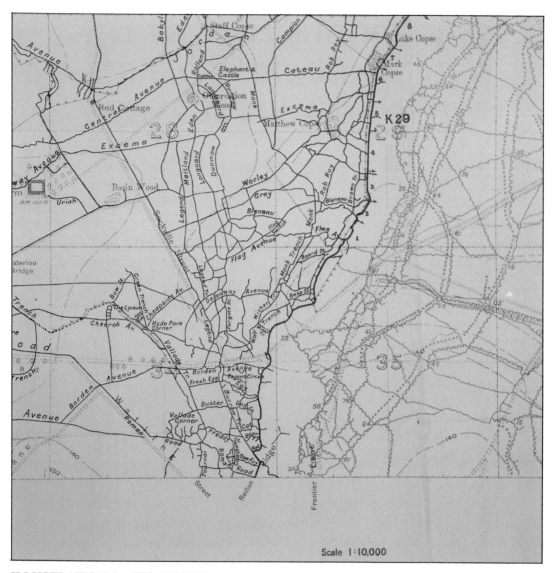

ILLUSTRATION 2   **WO 297/1470**
Opposing trench systems on the Somme, August 1916 (a portion of a 1:10,000 series Trench Map).

(c)   Maps that can directly advance genealogical knowledge by fulfilling function (a) above but also serving as graphic indexes to additional recorded information.

It is under this latter category that the Tithe, Valuation, and National Farm Survey maps and associated records fall.

A further example is the Bomb Census Maps (HO 193) which not only show the impact point of German bombs falling on the UK in the Second World War but provide references to the reports on those bomb strikes in the Bomb Census Papers (HO 198).

2. AN INTRODUCTION TO THE TITHE, VALUATION OFFICE AND NATIONAL FARM SURVEYS

Each of the land surveys is described in detail below. But, as an introduction for the family historian, it may be helpful to start by outlining briefly the value of these records. What sort of information can be obtained of use to genealogical research? And, because it is hoped as well that this guide will be read by the local historian and perhaps, as an introduction to these record sources, by the academic researcher, also included below are some notes on the wider significance of the records.

Essentially, the three surveys provide detailed snapshots of rural and urban landscapes during a hundred year period of great change in social and economic conditions. The Tithe surveys of 1836-c. 1850 were the most detailed examination of land use and land occupation since the Domesday Book of 1086. In turn, each of the following land and property surveys, that of the Valuation Office between 1910 and 1915 and the National Farm Survey, 1941 to 1943, was hailed at the time as the 'New' or 'Second' Domesday.

The maps generated by the surveys, and their accompanying records, provide information on the situation of individual property holders, the size of their landholdings and of their houses and gardens, the names and addresses of the landowners and the names of their tenants, with the amount of their rent. The Valuation Office records often give a physical description of houses and outbuildings, together with individual plans, and the National Farm Survey provides a detailed description of 300,000 farms and other agricultural holdings, recording virtually every animal and fruit tree. It can be seen that this information is of the greatest value to the family historian, enabling, for example, information of addresses obtained from the registers of births, marriages, and deaths (from 1837, available at the General Register Office), or from the census records made every ten years (beginning with the 1841 census, available at the PRO, Chancery Lane), to be greatly augmented. Put in simple terms, the different record sources allow us to match people with their homes and neighbourhoods, and to learn more about the conditions under which they lived.

Because of the enormous scope of the survey (*all* the land of England and Wales in the early twentieth century), the Valuation Office records are likely to be those most used by family historians. For the genealogist, the National Farm Survey will, of course, only be of interest if an immediate ancestor was a farmer or horticulturist.

The tithe records allow the family historian to venture back to the mid-nineteenth century. Fortunate genealogists will have three sources of information that will throw light on their ancestors and their places of abode across four generations.

From the local historian's point of view, the records assist in research into the history of particular properties, and enable a detailed picture of urban and rural communities to be built up, showing, for example, changes consequent upon the industrial revolution and the erosion of farming land to urban development. The Valuation Office records, in particular, can be of value in tracing rights of way (see page 41).

The historical geographer is presented with three massive databases of land and property ownership and of land usage during a period of critical agrarian revolution. The Valuation Office records, for example, provide a detailed record of both urban and rural settlement in the period just before the First World War, and the recent availability of the National Farm Survey records will enable comparisons to be made with farming conditions prevailing during the Second World War. The potential, in fact, for comparative work with the three different groups of records is enormous.

3. THE TITHE SURVEYS, 1836 - c. 1850[1]

Historical Background

Tithes - the payment by a farmer of one tenth of the annual production of his farm to maintain the established Church - had been in legal existence for over a thousand years. Originally, the custom had been a purely religious one, but it became state law in 855 AD during the reign of King Ethelwulf. In principle, payments were to be made in kind, ie every tenth basket of apples, every tenth fleece of wool, every tenth bushel of wheat, was to be paid to the parish priest for his own maintenance. Over the centuries, in some parishes payment by a fixed sum of money, or by a grant of land, had been substituted for the payment in kind. In particular, the Enclosure Acts of the eighteenth and early nineteenth centuries had been instrumental in extinguishing the obligation to pay tithes in kind.

However, in the opening decades of the nineteenth century, the great majority (some eighty per cent) of parishes were still paying tithes. This caused the greatest resentment to parishioners, who might be religious dissenters and did not see why the fruits of their efforts should support an established Church which put nothing itself into the business of farming. The tithe payers objected to the clergy growing rich as a direct result of their industry at a time when conditions were harsh for the farming communities. In addition, it seemed unfair that the farmers should have to meet this burden which was not shared, for example, by the artisans in the newly expanding industrial towns. Discontent and rural violence had reached such a peak by the 1830s that a Tithe Commutation Act was brought before Parliament in 1836. Under this Act, tithe payments in kind were replaced by a tithe rentcharge, which was paid in money in allotted proportion by all affected parishioners, by a set scale that was regulated according to the prevailing prices of corn calculated for the whole country.

To implement the Tithe Commutation Act, it was necessary to know the extent of existing tithe commutation and of the circumstances of each district where tithes were being paid. For this purpose, a Tithe Commission was established, and assistant commissioners travelled to all parts of the country to hold meetings with parishioners and settle the terms of the commutation of their tithes. These terms were formalized in a document called a *tithe agreement*, if all parties concurred, or a *tithe award*, if the assistant commissioner had to arbitrate in a dispute. The agreements or awards form the basis of the Tithe Apportionment, which records the landowners' individual liabilities and is supported by a large scale map showing each affected property. The Tithe Apportionments and Maps are essentially one single document, but for the convenience of use and storage they have been separated and now form two record classes, IR 29 (the Apportionments) and IR 30 (the Maps).

[1] The date c. 1850 is used as it was by this year that the great majority of the apportionments and their associated mapping consequent upon the Tithe Communication Act 1836 were completed.

6

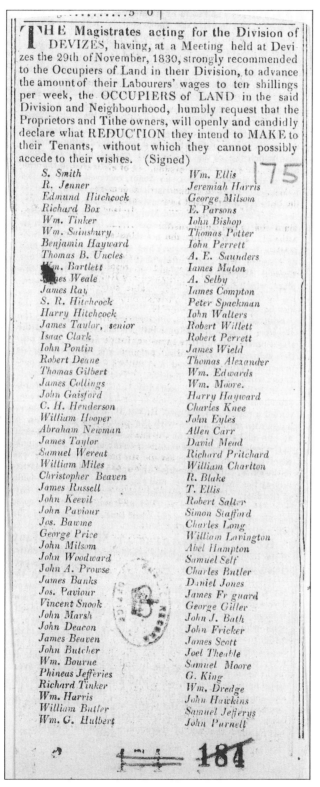

ILLUSTRATION 3   HO 40/27, f 175
Discontent at the payment of tithes. Pressure on tenant farmers to improve the lot of the agricultural labourer led to great resentment that the tithe owners themselves were not making any corresponding reduction in the burden of tithes. From the Correspondence and Papers of the Home Office relating to 'Disturbances'.

The Records and How to Use Them

The PRO holds approximately 11,800 Tithe Maps and the same number of Apportionments.

Readers will wish to use these records because they either require a large scale map of a neighbourhood in c. 1840 (as in the family history requirement set out on page 1) or because they wish to look for a particular individual living in a given parish (in which case they will need to examine the Apportionment as well as the Map).

The IR 29/IR 30 Class List

You should consult first the class list for IR 29/IR 30 to find the references to order the documents that you require (the references for both Apportionments and Maps are the same except for the IR 29 or IR 30 designation).

The class list is arranged alphabetically by the counties of England and then by those of Wales, and within each county alphabetically by the districts subject to tithe commutation. The type of tithe district (eg whether a parish, a hamlet, or a township) is indicated by an annotation alongside the place-name. Once you have found the district in which you are interested, take the number of the county from the top left of the page and add the relevant piece number from the left-hand column, viz the Tithe Apportionment for Fringford in Oxfordshire has the reference, IR 29/27/61, and the Tithe Map the reference, IR 30/27/61 (see illustration 4). Both Apportionments and Maps will be produced in the Map Room.

The Apportionments have all been filmed, and must be viewed on the microfilm viewers in the Map Room. If you have a valid reason to see the original document (for example, if the film is difficult to read), then you will need to allow two days for it to be brought from the PRO repository at Hayes.

As a conservation measure, there is a PRO programme of work to film in black and white all the Tithe Maps and make them available on fiche. Working alphabetically by county in the order of the class list, currently all have been filmed up to and including those for Middlesex. If the map you require is one of those that has been filmed, you will need to view it on one of the large fiche readers in the Map Room. Otherwise, the original map will be produced to you. It will normally be a rolled map, and you should take particular care how you handle it (see Chapter 7 on map care). The officer-in-charge of the reading room, or the repository manager, should be consulted for requests to see an original map in cases where the film is unclear or where distinctions made by differing colours are vital.

(27)	APPORTS. IR 29/(a)/(b)	
	MAPS IR 30/(a)/(b)	
	(a) COUNTY NO. (b) INDEX NO.	

OXFORD - CONTD.

Index No.	Tithe District and Description	Parish (where different from Tithe District)
	Fawler (see Charlbury)	
59.	Fifield (P)	
60.	Finmere (P)	
(61.)	Fringford (P)	
62.	Fulbrook (P)	
63.	Garsington (P)	
64.	Glympton (P)	
	Golder (see Pyrton)	
65.	Goring (P)	
	Gosford (see Kidlington)	
66.	Grafton (T)	Langford
	Great Haseley (see Haseley)	

ILLUSTRATION 4
Copy of part of a page from the IR 29/IR 30 class list showing the listing for Fringford in Oxfordshire. The county number and piece number have been ringed in this example.

The County Diagrams

If you cannot find the district you require in the class lists, the reason is very possibly that this parish or township was not subject to the Tithe Commutation Act (ie, as stated above, its tithes may have been extinguished earlier, possibly under one of the Enclosure Acts) and therefore no apportionment was drawn up. In the central reference cabinet in the Map Room are the three County Diagram volumes for England and Wales (see also their use under the Valuation Office records on page 27). In these volumes, the index maps for each county are coloured to show the parishes subject to the Tithe Commutation Act and those where tithes were extinguished under Enclosure Acts.

The Tithe Maps (IR 30)

The Tithe Commissioners, at the beginning of the surveys necessary under the Tithe Commutation Act 1836, tried to secure a uniform standard for the maps that were to form part of the tithe apportionment. The Assistant Commissioner, Lt R K Dawson RE, had been appointed to superintend the surveys, and he endeavoured to gain a uniformity in scale and the use of conventional signs. In bookcase 19 in the Map Room is a folder labelled 'Tithe Key' in which is a copy of Lt Dawson's recommendations on mapping standards and the types of conventional signs to be used.

However, the expense of the surveys, which usually had to be paid by the landowners, and the pressure of time, meant that it was not practicable to insist upon the same high standards being met everywhere. Consequently, the tithe maps differ greatly in scale and detail, although the predominant scales used for the large majority of maps varied between 3 to 6 chains to the inch (3 chains is about 25 inches to the mile). Some districts were mapped in full while others were only mapped for those parts subject to the tithe commutation. Largely because of the different scales, the size of the maps also varies considerably. Some are enormous, up to 14 feet in width and of a comparable length, while others, perhaps just concerned with a few fields, may measure 1 foot by 2 feet. The surveys took a long time to complete, and some districts were not mapped until the late 1840s.

Because of the varying quality of the maps, the Commissioners entered a provision into an amendment of the Tithe Act in 1837 that stated that only maps that were sealed as well as signed by the Commissioners could be termed 'accurate' and be deemed to represent an exact depiction of the particular land plots in question within a given parish. Such maps were known as 'first-class maps', and they number about 1,900 (some sixteen per cent only of the total).

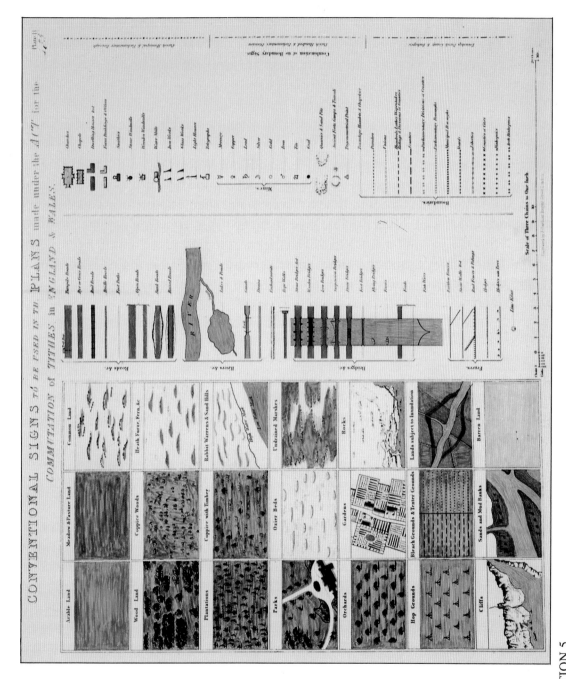

ILLUSTRATION 5
The conventional signs advocated by Lt Dawson for use on the tithe maps.

A recent four year research project undertaken by the University of Exeter has examined all the tithe maps in detail, and the results of that survey (showing for example the scope of a map, its scale, size, types of detail shown, whether coloured or not, conventional signs used, and the PRO reference) are now published as, Kain and Oliver, *The Tithe Maps and Apportionments of Mid-Nineteenth Century England and Wales* (Cambridge University Press, 1994). A copy is available for consultation in the Map Room, and readers are well advised to use this work in conjunction with the IR 29 and IR 30 class lists.

Although sometimes hard to interpret, and often demanding considerable local knowledge of the landscape, the tithe maps represent the earliest large scale mapping of most of the parishes of England and Wales and are an invaluable resource for local historians. It should be borne in mind that it was not only rural landscapes that were subject to tithes. Gardens and smaller plots of pasture within an urban context were often tithable, and so many urban areas are depicted in great detail. The expansion of many Victorian cities was to take place within a few years of the tithe surveys, and the tithe maps serve as well as a major record of a landscape of fields and woods soon to be overrun by brick and stone.

Tithe Area Numbers

An examination of a Tithe Map will show the reader that each land area subject to tithes is given a number, unique within the tithe district, and that number is shown on the map. As the information on land and property ownership is listed in the schedules of the Apportionment by those numbers, it is thus possible to cross reference from Map to Apportionment, and vice versa.

Tithe Maps Supplementary (IR 77)

Some original tithe maps were so heavily used that they fell into a bad state of disrepair. In most of these cases, the maps were copied by the Ministry of Agriculture and Fisheries, and it is these copies which are now in IR 30, while the originals, together with a few earlier versions of some tithe maps, are in the class of Tithe Maps Supplementary (IR 77). These number about one hundred, and Middlesex, Essex, Kent, and Surrey maps are represented in particular. As they are in poor condition, and, indeed, some are marked, 'Not Fit for Production', they should only be consulted if the maps in IR 30 fail to provide the required information.

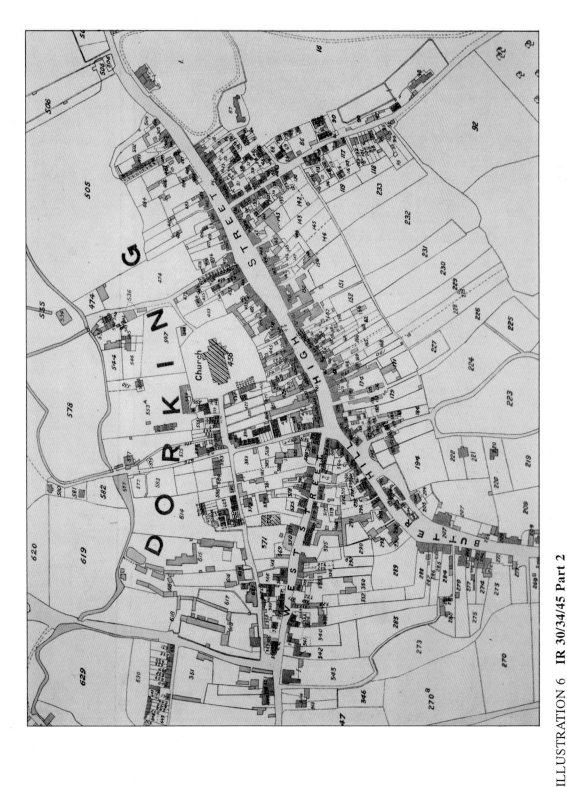

ILLUSTRATION 6 **IR 30/34/45 Part 2**
Part of the tithe map (reduced) for Dorking in Surrey, showing the centre of the town. Urban areas are sometimes included in great detail in the tithe surveys. This map is a 1927 copy of the 1838 original map, which can be found in the class of Tithe Maps Supplementary (IR 77/74). The latter, however, is in poor condition and will only be produced 'under supervision' (see also illustration 9).

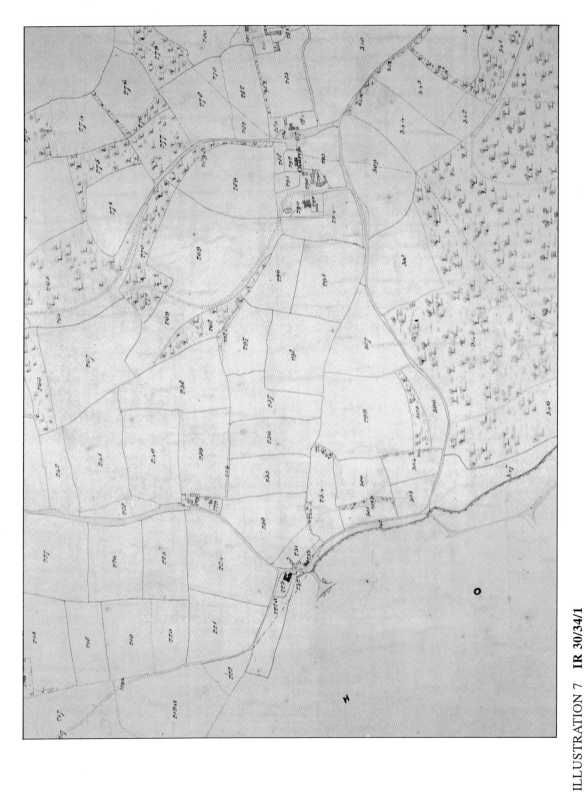

ILLUSTRATION 7   IR 30/34/1
A portion of the tithe map (reduced) of 1839 for Abinger in Surrey, showing the church and Abinger manor (area number 290). The position of the motte of the long vanished Norman castle is indicated by a dotted circle. At the edge of the map to the west lies the building (223) now the Volunteer Inn (see also illustrations 10 and 19).

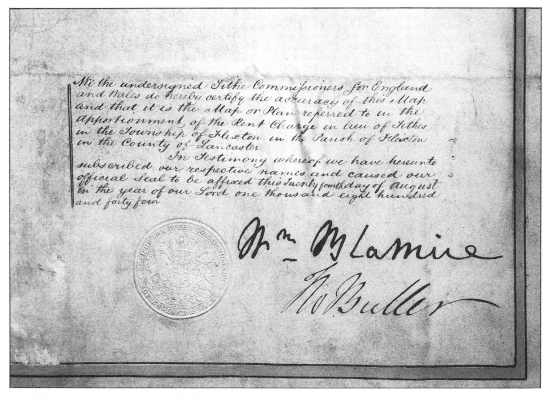

ILLUSTRATION 8   **IR 30/18/127**
The certification and seal of the Tithe Commissioners indicating a first class map. From the map for the township of Flixton in Lancashire.

The Tithe Apportionments (IR 29)

Unlike the Maps, the Apportionments generally follow a standard pattern. They are normally handwritten on parchment sheets, but in a few exceptional cases are printed (eg that for Widecombe in Devon, IR 29/9/449).

An Apportionment begins with a preamble reciting the names of the tithe-owners, and whether the amount of rentcharge to be apportioned was the subject of an agreement between the landowners and the tithe-owners or a compulsory award imposed by the Tithe Commissioners, and moves on to quote statistics as to the area and state of cultivation of the lands in the tithe district. Statistics are usually also given for the areas of commons and of roads, and for other lands exempt from tithes. The preamble generally ends with a statement of how the rentcharge will be calculated according to the prices of wheat, barley, and oats as prescribed by the Tithe Act 1837.

Next follows the main schedules of land and property ownership, which are set out in columns headed:

> Landowners
> Occupiers
> Nos. referring to the Plan
> Name and Description of Land and Premises
> State of Cultivation
> Quantities in Statute Measure
> Names of Tithe-Owners
> Remarks

You should therefore be able to discover the name of a landowner, the name of his tenant, the type of property he lived in, whether his land was ploughed or laid to grass, its area and extent, the amount of rentcharge he paid, and who to. The last column 'Remarks' is usually used to add abbreviations, for which there is a key obtainable from the officer on duty in the Map Room. These refer to the later history of the tithe rentcharge (see page 20).

The tithe area numbers do not necessarily run in consecutive order. The schedules are generally arranged alphabetically by the names of the landowners, and all the tithe areas under one landholding are placed together. These are often listed under the name of the farm or estate, and allow the extent of each landholding to be determined quickly. Sometimes extensive apportionments have an index to the tithe area numbers added, showing on which page of the apportionment each area appears. Such indexes do not form part of the original document, but have been added later for convenience of reference.

As stated earlier, it is not just farming land that was subject to tithes. The apportionments record houses, cottages, gardens, outbuildings, smith's shops, bake-houses and inns, and cover central urban areas as well as villages and agricultural landscapes.

The reader looking for the property of a particular ancestor will be able to search the appropriate Apportionment by the relevant surname. Otherwise, a search that seeks the name of the landowner of a particular property must start by identifying that property first on the Map, then noting its number, and turning to the schedules in the Apportionment.

C.—London: Printed and Published By Authority, by Shaw & Sons, 137 & 138, Fetter Lane.

OCCUPIERS.	Numbers referring to the Plan.	NAME AND DESCRIPTION OF LANDS AND PREMISES.	STATE OF CULTIVATION.	QUANTITIES IN STATUTE MEASURE.	PAYABLE TO Vicar.	PAYABLE TO Impropriators.	REMARKS and Names of Impropriators
				a. r. p.	£ s. d.	£ s. d.	
Himself and others (continued)	404	House Pleasure grounds &c	Brought forward	2 30			R 2396.
	405	House and garden		2 33			
	406	Workshop and Yard		11			
	407	House Workshop &c		37			
				1 3 12	3 10	4 "	
John Fedden	3193	Cottage Garden and Orchard		2 26	2 9		
Himself and another	11	Cottage and garden		3			
	124	d°		7			
Himself	150	Red Lion Inn Yards &c		3 6	3 9		R.18414.
Himself and others	196	House shop &c		7			
	1432	Beer shop House Garden &c		1 1			
	1610	Cottage		1			
	1619	d° and garden		24			
	1684	House and garden		1 19			
				3 12	1 6		R 2336 Coleman
Sarah Whitehouse and others	201	Workshops &c		1			
	204	House and garden		16			
	205	d°		20			
				37			
Himself and others	334	Cottage and Yard		3			
	335	d°		3			
	336	d°		6			
	337	Cottage		1			
	350	d°		1			
	359	Cottage and Yard		2			
	1603	House Garden &c		30			
	1684	Cottage and Garden		6			
	1685	d°		6			
				1 10			
Himself	954	House garden &c		3 2	9		48028.

ILLUSTRATION 9 **IR 29/34/45**
A page from the Apportionment of 1841 for Dorking (see illustration 6). The Red Lion Inn, a beer house, workshops, and cottages and gardens are listed with their owners' and occupiers' names.

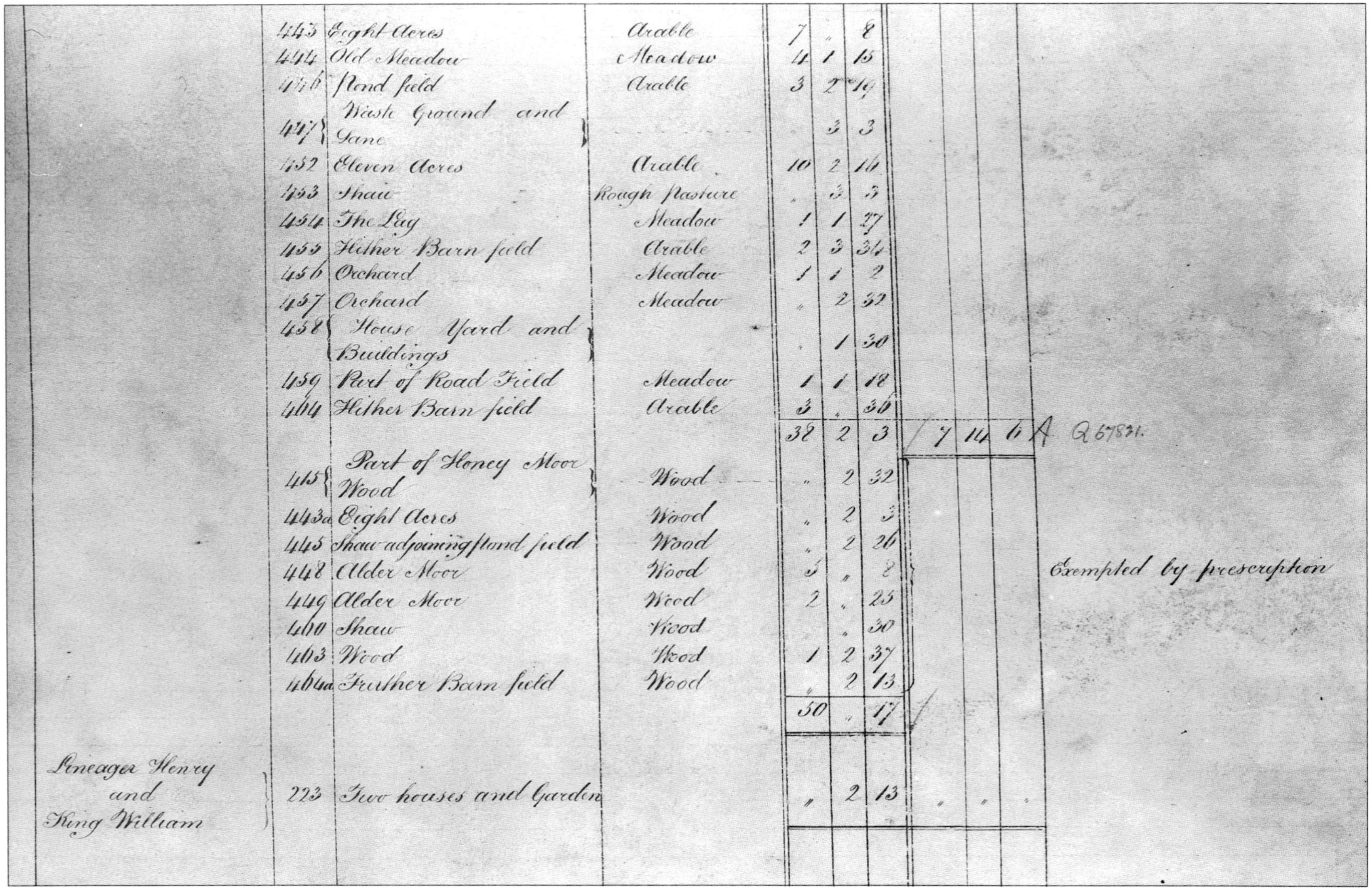

	443	Eight Acres	Arable	7	"	8				
	444	Old Meadow	Meadow	4	1	15				
	446	Pond field	Arable	3	2	19				
	447	Wash Ground and Lane			3	3				
	452	Eleven Acres	Arable	10	2	16				
	453	Shaw	Rough Pasture	"	3	3				
	454	The Lag	Meadow	1	1	27				
	455	Hither Barn field	Arable	2	3	34				
	456	Orchard	Meadow	1	1	2				
	457	Orchard	Meadow	"	2	32				
	458	House Yard and Buildings		"	1	30				
	459	Part of Road Field	Meadow	1	1	18				
	464	Hither Barn field	Arable	3	"	36				
				38	2	3	7	14	6	A Q 67831.
	415	Part of Honey Moor Wood	Wood	"	2	32				
	443a	Eight Acres	Wood	"	2	3				
	445	Shaw adjoining Pond field	Wood	"	2	26				
	448	Alder Moor	Wood	3	"	8				Exempted by prescription
	449	Alder Moor	Wood	2	"	25				
	460	Shaw	Wood	"	"	30				
	463	Wood	Wood	1	2	37				
	464a	Further Barn field	Wood	"	2	13				
				50	"	17				
Lineager Henry and King William	223	Two houses and Garden		"	2	13	"	"		

ILLUSTRATION 10 **IR 29/34/1**
Part of a page from the Apportionment of 1838 for Abinger (see illustration 7) recording area no. 223 as 'two houses and a garden' owned and occupied by Henry Lineager and William King. This property was to be developed later in the century as a public house, the Volunteer Inn (see also illustration 19).

Additional Records Resulting from the Tithe Commutation Act 1836

The Tithe Files (IR 18)

Correspondence and reports, including many plans, of the Assistant Commissioners' inspection of individual parishes and townships are contained in the class of Tithe Files (IR 18). These files are fullest where the commutation was in dispute, necessitating an award by the Commissioners. The contents of the files have been heavily weeded, but they survive for some 15,000 districts, including many parishes not subject to tithe commutation as the tithes had already been extinguished.

Tithe Awards and Agreements (TITH 2)

These are essentially the substance of the preamble to the Apportionment in IR 29, ie the reciting of the agreement, or, if in default of agreement, the award. Of interest to the family historian, however, is the fact that the documents contain the signatures of the landowners involved.

Boundary Awards (TITH 1)

Sometimes it was necessary for the Assistant Commissioners to define boundaries to resolve disputes between landowners as to tithe payments. The subsequent Boundary Awards include schedules of lands giving the names of owners and tenants, and are often accompanied by a plan.

Chancel Repairs

The record sources for the aspect of the tithe records that might involve the duty of repairing the chancel of a parish church are beyond the scope of this guide, and the reader is referred to PRO Records Information Leaflet 12 *Chancel Repairs,* where the sources and their use are described in full.

Tithe Records Held in Local Record Offices

An original and two copies of each Apportionment and accompanying Map were made in accordance with the provisions of the Tithe Commutation Act 1836. All copies were signed, and sealed where applicable, by the Commissioners.

The originals, which remained in the possession of the Tithe Commission, are those which are now in the PRO. The copies, which were deposited with the Registrar of the diocese and with the parish church, are now amongst the holdings of local record offices. Because, over the years, the copies have suffered neglect and loss, there are some gaps in these series of copy records. However, local archivists have been active in filling the gaps with microfilms made from the originals at the PRO.

Family historians contemplating a lengthy journey to the PRO to view Apportionments and Maps would be well advised first to consult their local record office as, essentially, all the required information should be available from the copies held locally. The above is not true, of course, of the additional records described on page 19.

The Further History of Tithes

The story of tithes subsequent to 1836-c. 1850 is long and complicated. As this guide is concerned primarily with the records generated by the Tithe Commutation Act 1836, no detailed attempt will be made to record that later history or to describe the subsequent tithe records. If you wish to try to trace the story of a tithe area further, using records available at the PRO, you should refer to Records Information Leaflet 41 *Tithe Records in the Public Record Office.* You should bear in mind that the Tithe Maps and Apportionments were documents used by the Tithe Commission until its dissolution in 1960, and then by the Inland Revenue until 1966, and they contain many later amendments and annotations. A key to the annotations in the 'Remarks' column of the Apportionment is available in the Map Room. The copies now deposited in local record offices (see pages 19-20) do not contain these later additions.

Briefly, the tithe rentcharge was ended, after further discontent and violence in the 1930s, by the Tithe Redemption Act 1936. Rentcharges were replaced by redemption annuities payable for sixty years. Owing to the high cost of administering these, they were extinguished by a final payment in 1977.

4. THE VALUATION OFFICE SURVEY, 1910 - 1915

Historical Background

The ownership of the majority of the land of Britain by a privileged few was seen by many in the early years of the twentieth century as a major cause of social injustice and poverty. The landed interest maintained great power in Parliament, and when the Liberal Government, of which Lloyd George was Chancellor of the Exchequer, introduced various land clauses into their 1909 Finance Bill, these were fiercely resisted. After initial rejection by the House of Lords, a twelve month struggle ensued and the Bill only reached the statute book after a further general election.

The Finance (1909-1910) Act 1910 provided for the levying of various duties on land, the principal one being 'Increment Value Duty'. This was to be levied at the rate of twenty per cent on the increase in the value of the land from its valuation as at 30 April 1909 until the occasion of its sale or other transference, the grant of leases for more than fourteen years, or the death of the owner. In the case of land held by corporate bodies, the increment value duty was to be calculated every fifteen years. However, farming land was exempted if it had no greater value than its current agricultural market value. House owners with land of less than fifty acres, and worth less than £75 an acre, were also exempted. The government's main concern was that private landowners should pay part of the increase in land values that was attributable, not to their own labour and efforts for improvements, but to expenditure by the state, for example in the provision of improved roads, drainage, and other public services.

In order to obtain the 'datum line' of information on land values as at 30 April 1909, Section 26(1) of the Act also provided for a valuation to be made of the land of the United Kingdom. This valuation included *all* property and land, whether it was later to be considered exempt or not. The valuation process, a 'New Domesday', would be of the greatest future assistance to the business of central government, helping with a reform of the rating system and in cases of compulsory purchase.

Many landowners did not cease their opposition to the Act's land clauses, and carried on their fight, mainly through the law courts where various test cases resulted in defeat for the government and challenged the whole basis of the valuation. The advent of the First World War interrupted the opposition to the land clauses, although the valuation process continued, but the clauses were finally repealed by the Finance Act 1920.

The valuation was carried out by the Board of Inland Revenue's Valuation Office, which had recently been set up to value property for the purposes of Estate Duty. In 1910 the establishment was only 61, and to carry out the valuation directed by the Finance (1909-1910) Act 1910 this staff was greatly expanded, both by permanent and temporary employees. By July 1914 it numbered some 600 permanent personnel, with an additional temporary 4,500 employees.

To provide for the physical execution of the valuation, England and Wales were divided into fourteen valuation divisions, which were subdivided into 118 valuation districts. Offices to accommodate the necessary staff to man these valuation divisions and districts were established.

The valuation process began during the summer of 1914. From August, landowners country-wide received what was to become the notorious Form 4-Land, which 'an owner of land or any person receiving rent in respect of land' was required to complete and return. Instructions on how to fill in the form were included. The penalty for not doing so was £50 (about £4,000 in modern values). By the end of the year approximately ten and a half million forms had been sent out and nine and a half million returned completed.

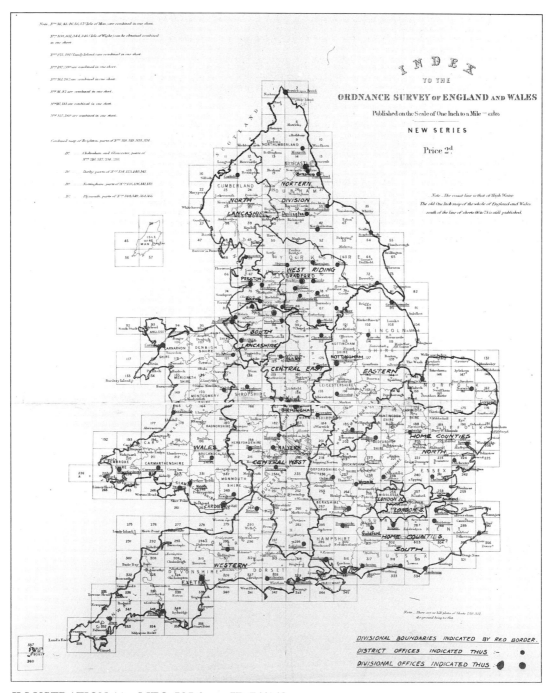

ILLUSTRATION 11   MFQ 535 from IR 74/148
The original Valuation Office divisions and districts used for the administration of the survey.

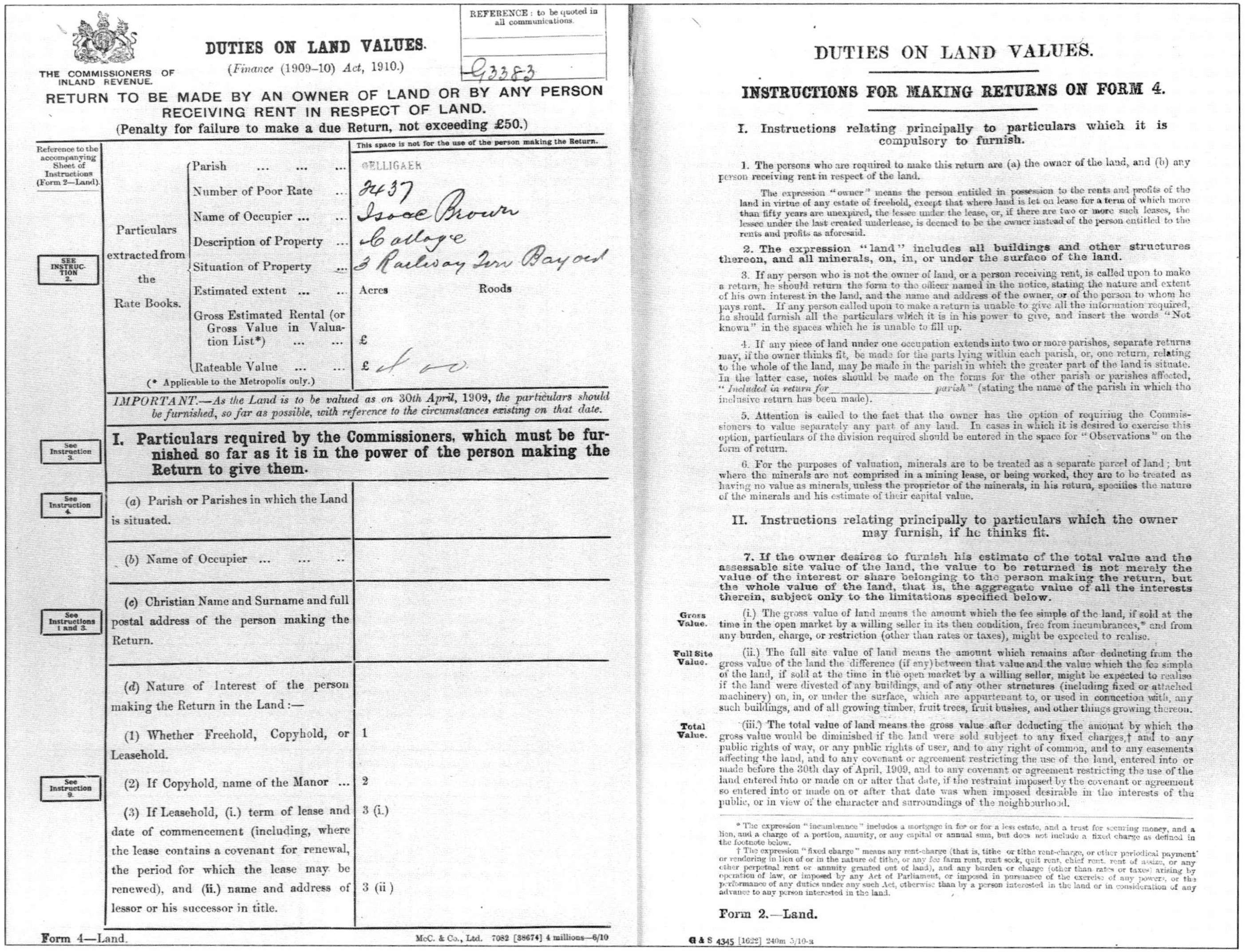

THE COMMISSIONERS OF INLAND REVENUE.

DUTIES ON LAND VALUES.

(*Finance* (1909–10) *Act*, 1910.)

REFERENCE: to be quoted in all communications. G3383

RETURN TO BE MADE BY AN OWNER OF LAND OR BY ANY PERSON RECEIVING RENT IN RESPECT OF LAND.

(Penalty for failure to make a due Return, not exceeding £50.)

Reference to the accompanying Sheet of Instructions (Form 2—Land).			This space is not for the use of the person making the Return.
SEE INSTRUCTION 2.	Particulars extracted from the Rate Books.	Parish	GELLIGAER
		Number of Poor Rate ...	2437
		Name of Occupier	Isaac Brown
		Description of Property ...	Cottage
		Situation of Property ...	3 Railway Terr Bargoed
		Estimated extent	Acres Roods
		Gross Estimated Rental (or Gross Value in Valuation List*)	£
		Rateable Value	£4 0 0

(* Applicable to the Metropolis only.)

IMPORTANT.—As the Land is to be valued as on 30th April, 1909, the particulars should be furnished, so far as possible, with reference to the circumstances existing on that date.

See Instruction 3. **I. Particulars required by the Commissioners, which must be furnished so far as it is in the power of the person making the Return to give them.**

See Instruction 4.	(*a*) Parish or Parishes in which the Land is situated.	
	(*b*) Name of Occupier	
See Instructions 1 and 3.	(*c*) Christian Name and Surname and full postal address of the person making the Return.	
	(*d*) Nature of Interest of the person making the Return in the Land:—	
	(1) Whether Freehold, Copyhold, or Leasehold.	1
See Instruction 9.	(2) If Copyhold, name of the Manor ...	2
	(3) If Leasehold, (i.) term of lease and date of commencement (including, where the lease contains a covenant for renewal, the period for which the lease may be renewed), and (ii.) name and address of lessor or his successor in title.	3 (i.) 3 (ii)

Form 4—Land. McC. & Co., Ltd. 7082 [38674] 4 millions—6/10

DUTIES ON LAND VALUES.

INSTRUCTIONS FOR MAKING RETURNS ON FORM 4.

I. Instructions relating principally to particulars which it is compulsory to furnish.

1. The persons who are required to make this return are (a) the owner of the land, and (b) any person receiving rent in respect of the land.

The expression "owner" means the person entitled in possession to the rents and profits of the land in virtue of any estate of freehold, except that where land is let on lease for a term of which more than fifty years are unexpired, the lessee under the lease, or, if there are two or more such leases, the lessee under the last created underlease, is deemed to be the owner instead of the person entitled to the rents and profits as aforesaid.

2. The expression "land" includes all buildings and other structures thereon, and all minerals, on, in, or under the surface of the land.

3. If any person who is not the owner of land, or a person receiving rent, is called upon to make a return, he should return the form to the officer named in the notice, stating the nature and extent of his own interest in the land, and the name and address of the owner, or of the person to whom he pays rent. If any person called upon to make a return is unable to give all the information required, he should furnish all the particulars which it is in his power to give, and insert the words "Not known" in the spaces which he is unable to fill up.

4. If any piece of land under one occupation extends into two or more parishes, separate returns may, if the owner thinks fit, be made for the parts lying within each parish, or, one return, relating to the whole of the land, may be made in the parish in which the greater part of the land is situate. In the latter case, notes should be made on the forms for the other parish or parishes affected, "*Included in return for* ________ *parish*" (stating the name of the parish in which the inclusive return has been made).

5. Attention is called to the fact that the owner has the option of requiring the Commissioners to value separately any part of any land. In cases in which it is desired to exercise this option, particulars of the division required should be entered in the space for "Observations" on the form of return.

6. For the purposes of valuation, minerals are to be treated as a separate parcel of land; but where the minerals are not comprised in a mining lease, or being worked, they are to be treated as having no value as minerals, unless the proprietor of the minerals, in his return, specifies the nature of the minerals and his estimate of their capital value.

II. Instructions relating principally to particulars which the owner may furnish, if he thinks fit.

7. If the owner desires to furnish his estimate of the total value and the assessable site value of the land, the value to be returned is not merely the value of the interest or share belonging to the person making the return, but the whole value of the land, that is, the aggregate value of all the interests therein, subject only to the limitations specified below.

Gross Value. (i.) The gross value of land means the amount which the fee simple of the land, if sold at the time in the open market by a willing seller in its then condition, free from incumbrances,* and from any burden, charge, or restriction (other than rates or taxes), might be expected to realise.

Full Site Value. (ii.) The full site value of land means the amount which remains after deducting from the gross value of the land the difference (if any) between that value and the value which the fee simple of the land, if sold at the time in the open market by a willing seller, might be expected to realise if the land were divested of any buildings, and of any other structures (including fixed or attached machinery) on, in, or under the surface, which are appurtenant to, or used in connection with, any such buildings, and of all growing timber, fruit trees, fruit bushes, and other things growing thereon.

Total Value. (iii.) The total value of land means the gross value after deducting the amount by which the gross value would be diminished if the land were sold subject to any fixed charges,† and to any public rights of way, or any public rights of user, and to any right of common, and to any easements affecting the land, and to any covenant or agreement restricting the use of the land, entered into or made before the 30th day of April, 1909, and to any covenant or agreement restricting the use of the land entered into or made on or after that date, if the restraint imposed by the covenant or agreement so entered into or made on or after that date was when imposed desirable in the interests of the public, or in view of the character and surroundings of the neighbourhood.

* The expression "incumbrance" includes a mortgage in fee or for a less estate, and a trust for securing money, and a lien, and a charge of a portion, annuity, or any capital or annual sum, but does not include a fixed charge as defined in the footnote below.

† The expression "fixed charge" means any rent-charge (that is, tithe or tithe rent-charge, or other periodical payment or rendering in lieu of or in the nature of tithe, or any fee farm rent, rent seck, quit rent, chief rent, rent of assize, or any other perpetual rent or annuity granted out of land), and any burden or charge (other than rates or taxes) arising by operation of law, or imposed by any Act of Parliament, or imposed in pursuance of the exercise of any powers, or the performance of any duties under any such Act, otherwise than by a person interested in the land or in consideration of any advance to any person interested in the land.

Form 2.—Land.

G & S 4345 [1622] 240m 5/10-a

ILLUSTRATION 12 **RAIL 1057/1714**

An example of the Form 4-Land (reduced) returned by the Rhymney Railway Company on behalf of one of their employees, Isaac Brown (with a page from the instructions for completing the form).

The information from the Form 4 return was transcribed into the valuer's Field Book, and a physical inspection of all properties was now made. Maps were also drawn up showing the position and extent of each property and plot of land to be valued. The inspection process was of necessity a most time consuming process. By 1912 the district Valuation Offices were running well behind the planned schedule, and instructions were issued to fulfil certain aspects of the survey more quickly. In particular, farms, which up to then had been recorded in great detail, often with plans in the Field Books showing all their buildings, were recorded far more summarily.

The commencement of the First World War, drawing off as it did many of the Valuation Office's staff, put an additional strain on the valuation process, but the main work of the original valuation was completed by the autumn of 1915, only six months behind the estimated date.

The Records and How to Use Them

The principal series of records held by the PRO of the Valuation Office survey of 1910-1915 are the Field Books (IR 58) and the Record Maps (see references below).

As described above, the information on each unit of property gained from the Forms 4 and by inspection in the field was recorded in the Field Books. A graphic index to these Field Books is provided by the Record Maps. These maps are Ordnance Survey sheets at various scales to which have been added, normally in red ink, hereditament (or assessment) numbers - one number for each property or parcel of land. The hereditament was the basic unit of valuation. Hereditaments were arranged within Income Tax Parishes (see page 43) which lay themselves within the Valuation Office districts.

You will need to find the right map sheet to locate the property in which you are interested, then make a note of its hereditament number and go to the Field Books where you will find a description of the property. Without the hereditament number, you will find it very difficult to locate the property in the Field Books. Consequently, the first step in any search is usually to find the relevant map sheet.

The Record Maps

Finding the Map Sheet (for maps of Central and Greater London, consult pages 33-34).
The Valuation Office maps are arranged by scale and by numerical order of
Ordnance Survey sheet reference in accordance with the administrative areas of
regional valuation offices (as they were in 1988). These thirteen Valuation Office
regions (altered considerably from the original fourteen 1910 divisions) are given
references (IR 121; and IR 124-IR 135), each of which is then sub-numbered by
alphabetical order of the district valuation offices within that region. One hundred
and thirty-five record classes of Valuation Office maps are thereby established (see
Appendix 1). The classes IR 125/6 (Portsmouth) and IR 125/10 (Southampton)
exist as references only because the maps they would have otherwise contained
were all destroyed by enemy bombing in the Second World War.

The standard Ordnance Survey scale used was 1:2500 (or 25 inches approximately
to the mile). However, the following scales were also used:-

1:10560	(6 inches to the mile) - used for moorland and upland areas of low population density.
1:1250	(50 inches approx. to the mile) - used for urban areas.
1:1056	(60 inches to the mile) - used for Central and Greater London.
1:500	(127 inches approx. to the mile) - used for densely populated town and city centres.
1:528	(120 inches to the mile) - used as the 1:500 series for a few small areas only; an older survey dating from the 1850s.

The date range of the main series of maps is approximately 1880 to 1915. However,
a few of the maps at the 1:528 scale date from the 1850s and some from the 1870s.
Irrespective of their Valuation Office content, the maps can also be used as a major
resource of Ordnance Survey large-scale plans of those date periods. The scale 1:2500
shows street names and that of 1:500 the names of larger detached houses.

You should bear in mind that the boundaries of the Valuation Office regions
and districts, and indeed of certain counties, have altered since the 1910-1915
survey and this can sometimes cause difficulty in locating the required map sheet.
Under certain circumstances, a measure of trial and error, together with some
perseverance, may be necessary.

If you have already acquired from another source (eg the Valuation Book - see page
50) the Ordnance Survey sheet reference that you need, then go straight to page 30.
If not, to find your required map sheet, you should proceed as follows:-

The County Diagrams (Key Sheets)

These are kept in the central map reference cabinet in the Map Room: their original purpose was to act as a guide to the areas receiving apportionments under the Tithe Commutation Act 1836 (see page 9), but they serve as well as a key to Ordnance Survey sheets at the 1:10560, 1:2500, and 1:1250 scales. IGNORE for this purpose the tithe information on the sheets, including the red manuscript numbers.

Vol 1 (Sheets 1-23)   Bedfordshire - Norfolk
Vol 2 (Sheets 24-43)   Northamptonshire - Yorkshire
Vol 3 (Sheets 44-55)   Wales: Anglesey - Radnorshire

Note

* **Hampshire** is filed in Vol 2 as Southamptonshire.
* For **Essex**, with the exception of the SW corner of the county, the Key Sheet is not applicable as this relates to the 'new series' of 1:2500 maps, and not the old series used principally by the Valuation Office. You should refer instead to the photocopy of the index sheet for the old series which has been added to the County Diagrams. The few 'new series' 1:2500 maps for Essex are included in IR 121/2 and IR 121/17, and the means of reference to these **is** the appropriate Key Sheet in Vol 1 above.
* For **Northumberland**, the Valuation Office used the old series maps for the entire county, and you should ignore the Key Sheet but use instead the photocopy index sheet to the old series that has been added.

1.   Consult the Key Sheet for the appropriate county.

2.   Find the place/area for which you require a map sheet. The Key Sheets are covered by a grid showing large numbered rectangles which are divided in turn into sixteen equal smaller rectangles (each of these represents a map sheet at the 1:2500 scale).

3.   1:2500 sheets
Take the printed number of the large rectangle into which the area you require falls. Next, count the number of small rectangles within that numbered rectangle to the one that covers your area more precisely (count in horizontal rows, left to right, from the top left-hand corner - as in the illustration below). Note that the numbers of the small rectangles are not actually given on the Key Sheets.

1	2	3	4
5	6	7	8
9	10	11	12
13	14	X 15	16

This provides the reference **31.15** for the indicated 1:2500 sheet.

4.   You must now convert the first part of the reference to Roman numerals (see PRO Records Information Leaflet 55 *How to read Roman numerals,* if you are not familiar with Roman numerals). **XXXI.15** is thus the Ordnance Survey sheet reference for the county in question that now needs to be keyed up with the appropriate class list (see page 30).

5.   1:10560 sheets
As the Valuation Office used maps at a number of scales (see above), you may need to note the references to those sheets as well.

If a 1:10560 (6 inch) sheet is required for the same place as in 3. above, then its reference will be **XXXI SE** (see illustration below). Four 1:2500 sheets make up the area of a 1:10560 sheet, and these areas within the large rectangle are denoted, NW, NE, SW, and SE.

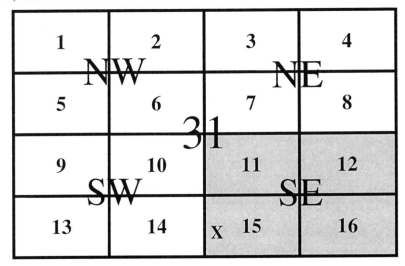

6.   1:1250 sheets

The sheet reference for the same place at the 1:1250 scale is **XXXI.15 SW**. The area of each 1:2500 sheet has to be considered as divided into four, and these divisions (each of which represents a 1:1250 sheet) are termed, NW, NE, SW, and SE (see illustration below).

1	2	3	4
5	6	7	8
9	10	11	12
13	14	NW / NE / SW / SE (15) X	16

7.   1:500 sheets

For the reference to a 1:500 sheet, the appropriate area covered by the 1:2500 sheet has to be considered as divided into twenty-five rectangles (five rows of five), each of which represents a sheet at the 1:500 scale (see illustration below). Because of the small scale of the Key Sheets, it is recommended that (where possible) the 1:2500 sheet be ordered first and this used as the key map to identify the 1:500 sheet reference required. A transparent grid overlay for this purpose is available from the officer on duty in the Map Room. The 1:500 sheet indicated has the reference, **XXXI.15.17.**

1	2	3	4	5
6	7	8	9	10
11	12	13	14	15
16	X 17	18	19	20
21	22	23	24	25

The Parish Indexes

These indexes are available for each county of England and Wales, and are bound into a single volume that can be found in bookcase B in the Map Room.

They provide an index to the county six-inch sheets that cover a particular parish, and will be useful when a place-name is not included on the County Diagrams (Key Sheets), or when you are not sure where within a county a particular place lies. The index provides the sheet number and its quarter, ie NW, NE, SW, or SE. Most parishes spread over more than one such six-inch sheet, but you will soon be able to pinpoint the exact sheet you require by ordering adjacent sheets until you have found the location of the property in question.

You can use the Parish Indexes as well to obtain the references of sheets at the 1:2500 scale by remembering that NW consists of 1:2500 sheets, 1, 2, 5, 6; NE, 3, 4, 7, 8; SW, 9, 10, 13, 14; and SE, 11, 12, 15, 16.

Note that the same problems with Essex and Northumberland sheets as are set out on page 27 apply equally to the Parish Indexes, and for most areas of Essex, and the whole of Northumberland, you should not use them.

The Class Lists (IR 121; IR 124 - IR 135)

Having obtained your map sheet reference, turn next to the class lists for the Valuation Office Record Maps (IR 121; and IR 124-IR 135). Appendix 1 is a list of the Valuation Office district offices arranged alphabetically within their regions, providing the PRO reference for each class of maps.

You need now to determine under which Valuation Office district your map falls and thereby in which PRO class it may be found.

1. Use Appendix 1 to identify the most likely class. In some cases this will be straightforward: in others you may have to select a number of possible options.

2. Appendixes 2 and 3 will be of assistance as they provide references to all relevant classes for a particular county or place. Appendix 2 includes the different scales available within each map class. You can also obtain from the officer on duty at the central podium position in the Map Room a further index of place-names that links the place directly to the PRO reference for the appropriate map sheet.

3. Quick Reference County Listings

If you have a sheet reference to a 1:2500 map of Cornwall, Devon, Dorset, Gloucestershire, or Hampshire, then you can go straight to the Quick Reference volume for those counties which is kept in bookcase B in the Map Room. This provides an immediate PRO reference for each 1:2500 sheet.

In addition, if part of the area of a 1:2500 sheet is also available at a larger scale, then this is indicated in the listing by an asterisk.

It is hoped eventually to make similar Quick Reference listings available for all the English and Welsh counties.

4.   The Index of Places (including street indexes for London) that forms part of the IR 58 (Field Books) class list may be of assistance. This provides under the head 'Valuation' the name of the Valuation Office district office for each 'Parish or Place'. However, be aware that this index relates to the Field Books rather than the maps and reflects an earlier (1950s) administrative arrangement of the Valuation Office. Consequently, it should be regarded as a help in suggesting the place-names of possible district valuation offices rather than as a direct key to the arrangement of the map classes (the two may not necessarily correlate).

5.   Look at the list for the class that you have selected and find the section under the relevant county which is at the scale you are seeking (most likely this will be at the 1:2500 scale, but very possibly sheets at the 1:1250, 1:500, and 1:10560 scales will be shown for that county in the list as well). The sections for each scale are normally arranged in the order given above, but this is not always the case and you should look through the list carefully to make sure you have identified the different scales for a particular county (Appendix 2 shows all the scales included within each class).

6.   The map sheet references run in numerical sequence for each section of the list. If you cannot find the sheet reference you want, then choose another of the class options you have selected and search that list under the correct county, and keep doing that until you have located the required sheet reference. From the left-hand column you will then be able to find the relevant piece number and so have the full document reference by which to order the map.

7.   Remember that, if you do not find the sheet you require under, for example, the 1:2500 scale, there may be a comparable sheet at another scale. Think whether the area you are seeking is within a large town or city, or whether it is in a sparsely populated area of the country, in which case the Valuation Office may have used 1:1250, 1:500, or 1:10560 sheets.

8.   If you cannot find the map sheet you require, you should bear in mind that the Record Maps are not necessarily complete. Those for Portsmouth and

Southampton, and an area around Chichester, were lost in the Second World War, and many in Essex in the neighbourhood of Chelmsford and the entire city area of Coventry appear also to be lost. Currently the PRO is listing a further 10,000 sheets, and a computer print-out of those sheets that fill gaps in the current listings is available from the officer in charge in the Map Room.

If you cannot locate the map sheet you require, all is not lost as the hereditament number may be available from the Valuation Book (see page 50).

This margin not to be used.	Reference IR 135/1	OS Sheet Reference	IR 135/1 VO Map Ref
		CARLISLE – contd	
		Cumberland – contd Scale: 1/10560	
	1067	LXXV NW	
	1068	LXXV NE	
	1069	LXXV SW	
	1070	LXXV SE	
	1071	LXXVI NW	
		Westmorland Scale: 1/2500	
	1072	III 12	
	1073	III 14	
	1074	III 15	
	1075	III 16	
	1076	IV 6	
	1077	IV 7	
	1078	IV 9	
	1079	IV 10	
	1080	IV 11	
	1081	IV 12	
	1082	IV 13	
	1083	IV 14	

ILLUSTRATION 13
Part of a page from the Valuation Office map class lists, showing how different counties and scales appear within the same class. The reference, for example, for the 1:2500 map, Westmorland IV.13, is IR 135/1/1082.

Finding Maps of Central and Greater London

The Ordnance Survey sheets used by the Valuation Office for the London area were those mapped at the 1:1056 scale (60 inches to the mile). The volume of Key Sheets that serves as an index to this series of map sheets is held in the central map reference cabinet in the Map Room with the County Diagrams. (Note that there are some London sheets for the Essex border areas at the 1:1250 scale in the classes IR 121/17 and IR 121/20: no Key Sheet is currently available for these).

1. When you have located the place you are seeking on the appropriate Key Sheet, take the reference number that is at the centre of the rectangle in which it falls, eg **10.69**. Convert the first part of the reference into Roman numerals, ie **X.69**. This is the London sheet reference that you require (see illustration below).

For some of the outlying areas of Greater London it may be necessary to order both the London sheet and that for the appropriate bordering county to find out which one contains the required Valuation Office information.

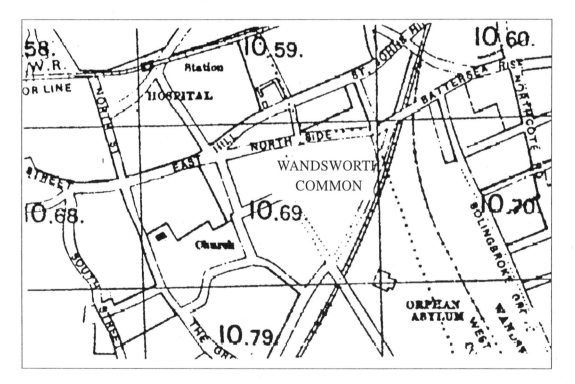

Extract from the Key Sheets to the 1:1056 map series for London. The map reference for the area of Wandsworth Common is 10.69 (X.69).

2. You now need to follow the same procedures as set out on pages 30-31. The London map sheets are in nineteen record classes under the reference of the Valuation Office London region, IR 121. When using the lists for these classes always check that you are looking under a 'London' head and at the 1:1056 scale (or, for two London sections in IR 121/17 and IR 121/20, the 1:1250 scale). The Index of London Parishes/Districts, and the London Street Index, that form part of the IR 58 class list may be of assistance in finding the Valuation Office district under which the map you require is filed.

Sheet X.69 in our example falls under the Merton Valuation Office district, class reference, IR 121/1. Sheet X.69 has the full reference, IR 121/1/29.

Explaining the Maps

1. The maps held by the PRO (some 70,000-80,000) are mostly the Record Maps or Record Plans, many mounted on linen, and intended as a permanent record of the hereditaments. Unlike the Working Maps (see page 51), they were kept in the district valuation offices and not taken into the field.

However, an inspection of many of the classes of maps does indicate that included in the PRO's holdings are many working maps. Often these are annotated with references, reflecting the later business of the Valuation Office as recent as the 1970s. There are many 'duplicates', indicated in the lists as 'parts', and, in such cases, it may be necessary to examine all the sheets as they are seldom exact duplicates, but do, in fact, vary considerably in the information that they contain.

Many of the maps are in a poor state of repair and should be handled with especial care (see Chapter 7). The PRO is currently undertaking a programme of work to conserve these, but the numbers involved are huge and it will be several years before the work is completed. If you note a map which is badly torn, or where the hereditament numbers and other cartographic details are peeling from the linen backing, then please inform a member of staff so that the map can be noted for conservation treatment.

2. The boundaries of the Valuation Office's administrative units for valuation purposes (the Income Tax Parishes (ITPs) - see page 43) are often shown on the maps in yellow, and the boundaries of each unit of valuation (the hereditaments) in pink or green. Sometimes the whole of each area of valuation is coloured with a full coloured wash. However, this practice was not universal, and the district valuation offices often used differing colours. Each unit of valuation, however, should have its boundaries emphasized by some form of colour marking.

3. Hereditament Numbers

The hereditament numbers are always those added to the map by the Valuation Office. Do not confuse them with the printed black Ordnance Survey land parcel numbers and acreage figures.

4. Where several detached parcels of land have a common owner and form a hereditament, each of these is shown on the map as a 'Part' or 'Pt.', eg 816 Pt. Sometimes the number of parts involved is given on the map (often shown as a figure in brackets after the hereditament and part number). Otherwise, the Field Books will provide a schedule of the parts using the Ordnance Survey parcel numbers and the acreage figures as references. The various parts may well extend over several map sheets within the ITP.

Separate parts of a hereditament adjoining across a common feature such as a road are usually shown joined together by a brace (normally in red ink). This is the same type of brace as used by the Ordnance Survey to link split parcels of land. Sometimes half-braces were used by the Valuation Office to emphasize the boundaries of part hereditaments.

5. When looking, for example, at a map of the 1:2500 scale, remember that there may also be sheets at the 1:1250 and 1:500 scales. If the property for which you seek an hereditament number is left blank, then it may be that this area has been covered by the Valuation Office at a larger scale, and you will need to seek the relevant 1:1250 or 1:500 sheet. This is particularly likely in the case of heavily populated urban areas.

It is useful to remember this point if you are simply using the Valuation Office maps as a resource of large scale Ordnance Survey plans. The cartographic information on the 1:1250 sheets is identical with that from the 1:2500 survey as the former is purely a photographic enlargement of the latter. The increased scale, however, may make certain details clearer. The 1:500 sheets are of an entirely separate survey and contain a great deal of additional detail, including the exact block plans of buildings, the lay out of gardens, the width of street pavements, and even the position of individual and roadside trees.

6. When looking for a map of a 'new county' created in 1974, search under the former name/s of that county. A sheet showing the county alterations at that date is available from the officer on duty in the Map Room. If you cannot find a map for an area at the borders of a county, remember to look as well under the adjacent county.

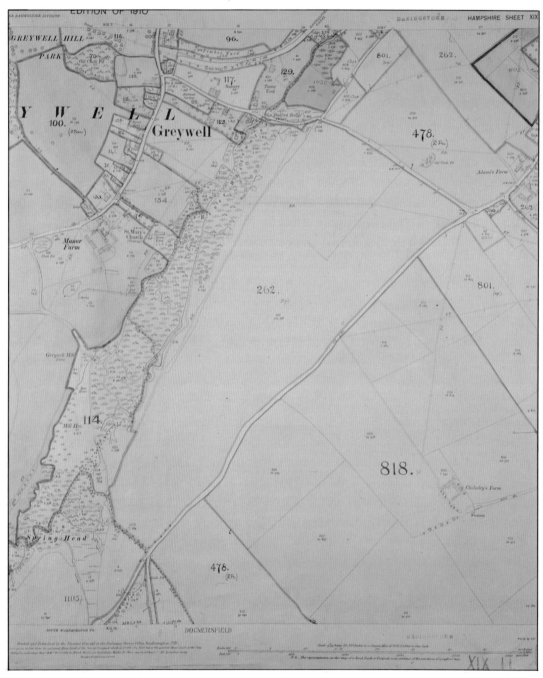

ILLUSTRATION 14   **IR 125/4/151**
A part of 1:2500 Ordnance Survey sheet, Hampshire XIX.11 (reduced), showing the village of Greywell. The names of both the district Valuation Office, Basingstoke, and that of the Income Tax Parish of which Greywell is a part, Dogmersfield, are given in the margins. This map shows as well the recording of the different parts of an hereditament, and the way certain parts may be bracketed together.

ILLUSTRATION 15   **IR 126/8/127**
Portion of the Valuation Office record sheet (reduced) for St Albans, Hertfordshire XXXIV.7 at the scale 1:2500, showing how the central city area is without hereditament numbers, but has the annotation, 'see enlarged sheet'. The Valuation Office has, in fact, used 1:1250 scale sheets to show these crowded hereditaments in the detail required (see illustration 16).

37

7. If you need to order a map sheet immediately adjacent to the one that you are using, remember that the Ordnance Survey references for the neighbouring sheets are given at each border of the map. You will then be able to key up these sheet references with the appropriate class list to obtain the necessary PRO reference.

8. If you have already obtained an hereditament number from another source (eg the Valuation Book - see page 50) and are seeking the relevant map, then note that the Field Books often give the map sheet reference against the hereditament number on the first page of the entry.

9. Sometimes the top of a map sheet will be stamped with a place-name (usually in red), or this name will have been added in manuscript. Sometimes as well, the place-name is added after the hereditament number. This is the name of the Income Tax Parish (ITP) (see page 43) under which the area of the map fell. It may be vital to have this information when you are seeking a Field Book.

ILLUSTRATION 16   **IR 126/8/257**
Portion of the 1:1250 record plan, Hertfordshire XXXIV.7 SE , showing hereditaments in the central area of St Albans. A description of each of these hereditaments may be obtained in the relevant Field Book.

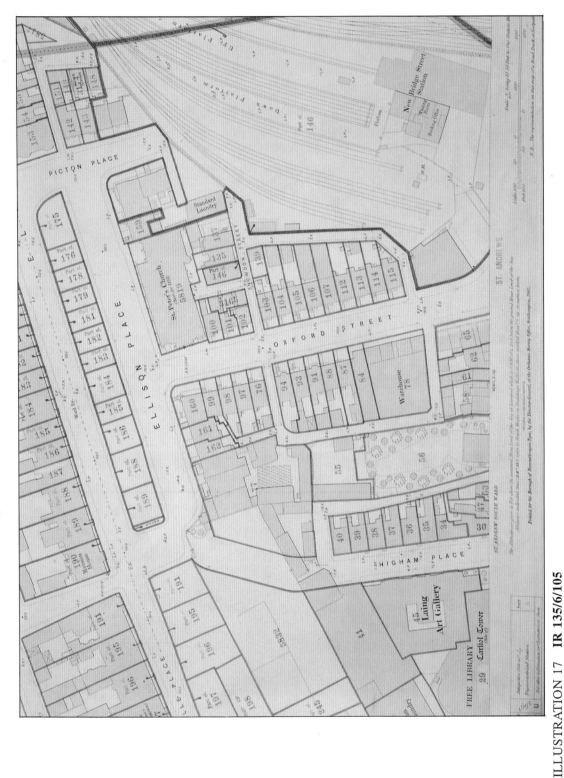

ILLUSTRATION 17   IR 135/6/105
For the most densely populated urban areas, the Valuation Office used the enormous 1:500 scale. This is a portion (reduced) of a record plan for Newcastle upon Tyne, XCVII.7.5.

The Field Books (IR58)

Finding and Using the Field Book

Having obtained your hereditament (assessment) number, you now need to look at the class list to IR 58 to obtain the PRO reference to the relevant Field Book.

The Field Books (IR 58), which are of standard size - 6" by 10" and 1" thick, contain the information on each hereditament recorded by the valuers. They are arranged by numerical sequence of hereditament numbers, with four pages to each hereditament and up to 100 hereditaments to a Field Book. The amount of information varies considerably, but you might hope to find the full street address of the property, an interior and exterior description (including the number and use of rooms and the state of repair, and sometimes a detailed plan), the name of the owner and of the occupier, the date of construction and of any previous sales, and the valuation figures, as well as a schedule of all neighbouring lands owned. Farms are often described and planned in great detail. Sometimes as well public buildings, such as town halls, churches, cathedrals, and historic buildings are recorded in a detail that seems far beyond the actual requirements of the survey. In the urban landscape, descriptions of factories, gas works, banks, hotels, and schools can be obtained. Sometimes the existence of public rights of way over the land is indicated in the valuation deductions column, and occasionally these rights of way are described, with the Ordnance parcel numbers given of the fields through which they pass.

The Field Books are arranged in accordance with the Valuation Office administrative areas as they existed in the 1950s. They number about 95,000. Those for the Portsmouth area, Winchester, and most of Southampton and Chichester, were lost to enemy action in the Second World War.

The Index of Places

1.   Use the Index of Places in England and Wales (and the Supplementary Index of Parishes), or the Index for London (arranged by street names and also by parishes/districts), which form part of the IR 58 class list. These will provide you, under the column headed 'Valuation', with the name of the Valuation Office district for the place where your property lies. Please note that parts of this index are not in the strictest alphabetical order, and you may need to check above and below the point where the place-name should be listed.

The IR 58 Class List

2. Go now to the IR 58 class list, which is arranged alphabetically by the Valuation Office districts, and then, within each district, alphabetically by ITP (see page 43). Find the volume which includes the Valuation Office district that you have obtained from the Index. The district names are given at the top of each page, and underneath in alphabetical order is the list of ITPs where you will hope to find the place-name that you seek.

3. Having located the correct name, take the range of hereditament numbers from the right-hand column that includes the hereditament number you obtained from the map. The left-hand column on the page will now provide you with the piece number for the required Field Book. To order this, you will need a seat number in the main reading room, but the Field Book will be produced in the Map Room.

	Reference		IR 58
	IR 58	HULL	
This margin not to be used.		Place Name	Assessment No.
	41193	Burstwick – contd.	101 – 200
	41194	"	201 – 300
	41195	"	301 – 335
	41196	Burton Pidsea	1 – 100
	41197	" "	101 – 200
	41198	" "	201 – 300
	41199	" "	301 – 400
	41200	" "	401 – 500
	41201	" "	501 – 540
	41202	Catfoss (Sigglesthorne)	1 – 94
	41203	Catwick	1 – 73
	41204	Cherry Burton	1 – 100
	41205	" "	101 – 116
	41206	Cottingham	1 – 100
	41207	"	101 – 200
	41208	"	201 – 300
	41209	"	301 – 400
	41210	"	401 – 500
	41211	"	501 – 600

ILLUSTRATION 18

Part of a page from the IR 58 class list. The Field Book for hereditament 114 in Cherry Burton, for example, has the PRO reference IR 58/41205.

The Income Tax Parish

4. If the place that you are seeking does not appear under the relevant district head in the IR 58 list, the likely reason is that it forms but part of an Income Tax Parish (ITP), the basic administrative unit for valuation within each Valuation Office district. An ITP can consist of a single civil parish, part of a civil parish, or several civil parishes. In the latter case, the ITP was known by the name of the first parish on the list which was often (but not always) arranged alphabetically. The hereditaments are numbered within each ITP and those numbers are unique to it.

An example of an Income Tax Parish is that headed by the civil parish of Alton in Hampshire, but which consists additionally of the parishes of Binstead, Chawton, Dockenfield, Farringdon, Newton Valence, Shalden, and East Tisted. Only the name, Alton, is given in the IR 58 class list, and the hereditaments of the other parishes will be found under that head, but are not separately shown.

You may find the name of the ITP in which your parish falls either:-

a. by looking at the relevant map sheet: often the name is stamped at the top, or has been added in manuscript (sometimes after the hereditament number) - see also page 38; or

b. by consulting the Board of Inland Revenue's *Alphabetical List of Parishes and Places in England and Wales* (obtainable from the central map reference cabinet in the Map Room). This volume may provide the name of the ITP in the first column headed, 'United with or included in' against the parish name. However, as the volume is dated 1897, and there were many alterations to the composition of ITPs over the years, the correct information will not be found in every case.

If neither of the above sources provides the ITP name, then you will need to use your local knowledge to search the IR 58 list under the names of other likely adjacent places. You will be able to discard any places whose ranges of hereditament numbers are not as high as the one you are seeking. A certain amount of trial and error will be inevitable.

The appropriate Valuation Book (see page 50) is the best source for the composition of an ITP. The Valuation Book will record all the parishes making up the ITP, and give the range of hereditament numbers for each such parish. If you cannot locate the Field Book required by any of the methods described above, then it may be necessary to visit the relevant local record office to consult the Valuation Book.

5. For very large properties and estates, the Field Books often did not contain enough space to include all the necessary details of these hereditaments. For such cases, the Valuation Office created special files (to which the Field Books refer, often in the form, 'description filed'): it is not thought that any such files have survived. The practice of making the major record of hereditaments outside the Field Book was carried out by certain valuation offices regardless of the size of the properties and land involved. For such properties, the sparse details in the Field Books can perhaps be supplemented by the Valuation Books and Forms 37 (the latter sometimes had additional details of large estates attached) - see pages 50-51.

6. Four sets of valuation figures are given for each hereditament. These were arrived at after a series of complicated calculations, which can be simplified as follows:-

Gross Value

The amount which the land might be expected to make on the open market, free of any encumbrances.

Full Site Value

The amount which remains after deducting from the gross value of the land the value of the buildings on it.

Total Value

The gross value, with deductions made for fixed charges, rights of way, and rights of common.

Assessable Site Value

The total value, with the same deduction made as to arrive at the full site value from the gross value, but with additional deductions for work and expenditure made by the owner to improve the land. It was on the assessable site value that increment value duty was payable.

30 ...... Reference No. ....

Situation _Sutton Abinger_ Map No. XXX.11.19 ⟨_The Volunteer Inn_⟩

Description _Beer House_ {_2 Cottages_}

Extent _2 roods 24 perches_

Gross Value {Land £ _10-15_ Rateable Value {Land £
⎨Buildings £ ⎬ ⎨Buildings £

Gross Annual Value, Schedule A, £

Occupier _Mr Mello_

Owner _Lucello, Huber & Co_

Interest of Owner _Freehold_

Superior interests

Subordinate interests

Occupier's tenancy. Term _Monthly_ from

How determinable

Actual (or Estimated) Rent, £ _22-10 including 2 cotts_

Any other Consideration paid .... paid by

Outgoings—Land Tax, £ .... paid by

Tithe, £

Other Outgoings

Who pays (a) Rates and Taxes (b) Insurance _(a occupier) (b owner)_

Who is liable for repairs _do_

Fixed Charges, Easements, Common Rights and Restrictions

Former Sales. Dates

Interest

Consideration

Subsequent Expenditure

Owner's Estimate. Gross Value

Full Site Value

Total Value

Assessable Site Value

Site Value Deductions claimed

Roads and Sewers. Dates of Expenditure

Amounts

Reference No. ....

Particulars, description, and notes made on inspection 21/8/13.

Details—brick & slate country inn. Ist floor Tap room Bar Parlour (little living room) General shop cellar (has only two shops) scullery towards ... well water only. Bath. Closet in farm. Public urinal. Above 5 bedrooms in ... indifferent repair. At rear 2 old cottages in cement brick whitewashed tile each containing a room and a scullery on the ground floor & 2 rooms over one

Charges, Easements, and Restrictions affecting market value of Fee Simple

Has also a ... they are let @ 2/- & 2/6 each respectively. There are 2 earth closets in the garden. ... an old urinal. The public house has a good garden with a timber built workshop in ...

Valuation.—Market Value of Fee Simple in possession of whole property in its present condition

Fee Simple value as per Mr Flete S.O. Report £950.   150

        1100

Add for 2 old cottages

Deduct Market Value of Site under similar circumstances, but if divested of structures, timber, fruit trees, and other things growing on the land

65 acres @ £100 an acre say £65   £ 65

Difference Balance, being portion of market value attributable to structures, timber, &c. .... £ 1035

Divided as follows:—

Buildings and Structures .... £ 1035

Machinery .... £

Timber .... £

Fruit Trees .... £

Other things growing on land .... £

Market Value of Fee Simple of Whole in its present condition .... £ 1100

Add for Additional Value represented by any of the following for which any deduction may have been made when arriving at Market Value:—

Charges (excluding Land Tax) .... £

Restrictions .... £

GROSS VALUE ... £ 1100

ILLUSTRATION 19   IR 58/69460
Part of the Field Book entry (hereditament 30 in Abinger ITP) for the Volunteer Inn, Sutton Abinger (see also illustrations 7 and 10). Some 75 years after the tithe survey, the property is now described as a 'beer house', but also in the same entry as a 'country inn' and a 'public house'.

Index letter	Description of Buildings	Dimensions			Cubical Contents	Condition	Remarks
		Frontage	Depth	Height			

...........................Reference No.

Small marble font, w. end of N. Aisle. Royal Pews Bristile annexe with entrance porch & stairs leading to 2 large front pews each with fireplace + 4 Pews at back. enriched plaster ceiling, front of pew classic style with Corinthian columns in rather low repair. The church is electrically lighted & heated by hot water radiators.

West end of N. Aisle Large Marble memorial to Leopold & Charlotte left hand panel depicts "Death of Princess Charlotte 6 Nov 1817, Centre panel "They visited the fatherless widows in their affliction" 2nd May 1816 Right hand panel Belgium offering the Crown to Prince Leopold & Britains acquiescing 1831 Executed by Williamson to 1860 & removed from Claremont. There are a large number of memorial tablets to local residents. The Church is not regularly used for Divine Service

ILLUSTRATION 20   IR 58/87890
Often the valuers went far beyond the requirements of the survey in the descriptions they provided of certain buildings. Here, a very full word-picture is given of the redundant St George's Chapel at Esher in Surrey where Queen Victoria had worshipped. It was valued at £3000 in view of its 'historical and sentimental interest'.

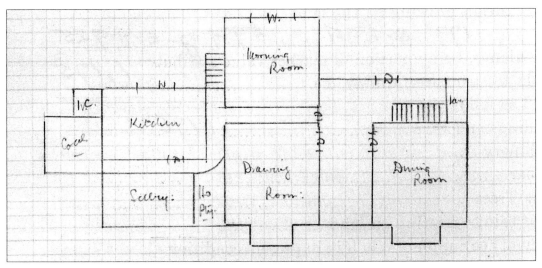

ILLUSTRATION 21   IR 58/14055
Plans in the Field Books record buildings often long since demolished. This plan is of a Victorian villa in Church Road, Shortlands (Beckenham ITP), pulled down in the mid-1970s.

Index letter	Description of Buildings	Dimensions			Cubical Contents	Condition	Remarks
		Frontage	Depth	Height			
	House .			26		Fair	Brick & tiles
	6 stall 5 stall & 3 stall cowhouse			14		Do	Do
	5 stall stable & calf houses			15		Do	Do
	covered shed .			16		Do	Do
	Barn Cartshed &c			18		Do	Do
	Blacksmiths shop			12		Do	Do
	Trap house .			12		Do	Do
	loose box .			12		Do	Do
	Meal house & piggeries			14		Do	Do

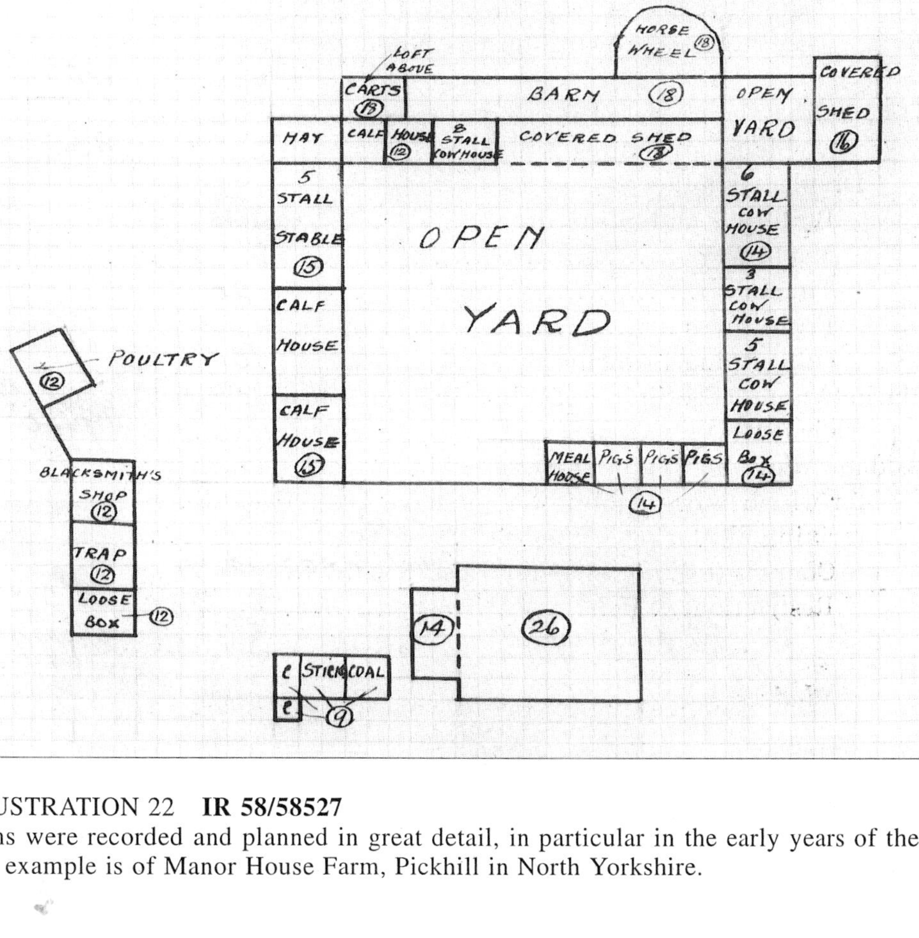

ILLUSTRATION 22   IR 58/58527
Farms were recorded and planned in great detail, in particular in the early years of the survey.
This example is of Manor House Farm, Pickhill in North Yorkshire.

47

379 ...... Reference No.   Map. No. ....   Reference No. ....

Situation ... Batemans

Description ... House, Bldgs & gdn

Extent ... 6.3.5

Gross Value { Land £ / Buildings £ }   Rateable Value { Land £ 110 / Buildings £93.10.0

Gross Annual Value, Schedule A, £

Occupier ... Rudyard Kipling "Batemans" Burwash Sx

Owner ... Do   freehold

Interest of Owner ... freehold

Superior interests

Subordinate interests

Occupier's tenancy, Term .... from

How determinable

Actual (or Estimated) Rent, £

Any other Consideration paid

Outgoings—Land Tax, £ 5.8.0   paid by ... Occupier

Tithe, £ 1.11.4   paid by ... Occupier

Other Outgoings

Who pays (a) Rates and Taxes (b) Insurance ... Occupier

Who is liable for repairs ... Occupier

Fixed Charges, Easements, Common Rights and Restrictions

Former Sales. Dates ... Purchased July 1902 last Feb 1905

Interest

Consideration

Subsequent Expenditure £1200

Owner's Estimate. Gross Value

Full Site Value

Total Value

Particulars, description, and notes made on inspection

A detached Stone & tile house of Jacobean period, but in 1634.
Stone mullioned windows & oak panelled & beamed.
Electric light installed
G.Fl. Hall (3pa) Dining room Library Boudoir Staircase
Scullery store room Lavatory Laid'd hair Le ondery staircase
1st Fl. 6 Bedrooms Dressing room fitted with Bathroom Bathrm
2nd Fl. 5 Bedrooms store room Servant's room Cupboards Radiators

Charges, Easements, and Restrictions affecting market value of Fee Simple
Well laid out lawns Ornamental lake Trout lawn
B+T Boathouse Cottage containg 6 rooms B+T note room
RangeB+T Bldg. Accumulator room — shed 1 B.T. high...
WC+T potty shed & & 2 glasshouses walled in kitchen gdn
Electric light installed, power being supplied by water from...

Valuation.—Market Value of Fee Simple in possession of whole property
in its present condition   Say 380,384

                                                            Now £200

                                                 Gut 200 wet
                                                            X 30 ryp   £6000

14.1.5   @ £35 14a.1a.5p @ £35 £500

Deduct Market Value of Site under similar circumstances,
but if divested of structures, timber, fruit trees, and
other things growing on the land

Difference Balance, being portion of market value attributable to structures, timber, &c. £5580

Divided as follows:—

Buildings and Structures .... £ 5470

Machinery .... £ 20

Timber .... £ 20

Fruit Trees .... £ 10

Other things growing on land .... £

ILLUSTRATION 23   **IR 58/29280**

The homes of the famous were recorded. This is part of the entry for the house, Batemans, in Sussex, showing the name of the owner (from July 1902), Rudyard Kipling (Hereditament 379 in Burwash ITP).

Reference No.....................

Particulars, description, and notes made on inspection

Brook Street Schools. This building is used as a dayschool in the week days and as a Chapel & Sunday School on Sundays. Built of brick, with slated roof, in moderate repair but the rooms are low and somewhat dark. and does not meet with the approval

~~Charges, Easements, and Restrictions affecting market value of Fee Simple~~ of B education people. There are 2 floors, with usual conveniences.

Valuation.—Market Value of Fee Simple in possession of whole property
   in its present condition

   29150 c.f. @ 4   485
              Site   30
                          515

                     say £   530

Deduct Market Value of Site under similar circumstances,
   but if divested of structures, timber, fruit trees, and
   other things growing on the land

   Site   2307 do @ 2/6   £   30

Difference Balance, being portion of market value attributable to structures, timber, &c. ....£   500

   Divided as follows:—
      Buildings and Structures.....................£
      Machinery ....£
      Timber...£
      Fruit Trees ....£
      Other things growing on land ....£

Market Value of Fee Simple of Whole in its present condition
   (as before) ....£

Add for Additional Value represented by any of the following
   for which any deduction may have been made when
   arriving at Market Value:—
      Charges (excluding Land Tax)..............£
      Restrictions..£   £

                              GROSS VALUE...£

ILLUSTRATION 24   **IR 58/24465**
The hereditaments of public buildings, churches, and schools in city centres are generally numbered successively. Hence, they can often be found together in one Field Book. An example is Congleton in Cheshire, where the city schools and churches are numbered 3461-3483. This example, the description of Brook Street School, Congleton, states that it 'does not meet with the approval of the education people' owing to its low, dark rooms.

Additional Records of the Valuation Office Survey

The Valuation Office survey (1910-1915) generated an enormous amount of paperwork: some 180 forms are said to have been used! The principal surviving documents (where this can be assessed) are as follows:-

Valuation Books

These volumes are sometimes known as 'Domesday Books', and, with two exceptions, are held by the relevant local record offices. The exceptions are the books for the City of London and Westminster (Paddington) which are held by the Public Record Office in the record class IR 91.

The Valuation Books were the first major record of the hereditaments created by the Valuation Office at the commencement of the survey. They record much of the same information as is in the Field Books, but without the detail of the survey in the field (ie the descriptions and plans of land and property), and often without the assessable site value figures. Sometimes the Valuation Books include the addresses of landowners when they were not the occupiers of that land.

The Valuation Books are particularly important because they can enable a hereditament number to be found when the map has not survived. All the parishes making up an Income Tax Parish are listed in the Valuation Book, and the composition of the ITP is normally given on the cover of the book and is often listed as such by the local record office. This can make it straightforward to find the ITP in which a particular parish lies. The hereditaments are listed in numerical sequence, parish by parish, for the whole ITP. Sometimes the Valuation Books for urban areas contain detailed indexes of street and house names, and it is therefore possible to find an hereditament by its street address. As stated on page 38, the Valuation Books usually contain the map reference where each hereditament can be found. The Valuation Books were used by the district valuation offices for long after the repeal in 1920 of increment value duty, and they often include later amendments recording, for example, change of ownership.

The Hampshire County Record Office holds Valuation Books for certain of the areas for which there are no Field Books owing to their loss in the Second World War, in particular areas of Winchester and Southampton.

Forms 37

These forms contained the record kept by the district valuation offices of the provisional valuation of each hereditament. They are important because they give detail of the exact area of each unit of land being valued, information which is not necessarily available in the Field Books. They also contain the addresses of landowners who were not owner/occupiers. A landowner could opt to have his land assessed by part hereditament, and the Form 37 is the only document that shows that part valuation that can be tied exactly to the Record Maps. Sometimes as well, additional details of large estates not included in the Field Books can be found attached to a Form 37 (see also page 44). Where they have survived, Forms 37 are held by local record offices.

Working Maps

Many of the local record offices hold copies of the Valuation Office's working maps - that is, Ordnance Survey sheets with the added hereditament numbers similar to the Record Maps held by the PRO. The working maps have often been used by the valuers in the field, and they may, therefore, include many pencilled comments and other markings relating to the hereditaments. If the PRO does not hold your required map sheet, then you should check at the relevant local record office to see if they have that sheet amongst their copies of the working maps.

Forms 4-Land

These forms, which were completed by the landowners and returned to the district valuation offices (see page 22), were not retained by the Valuation Office as a permanent record of the hereditaments. They appear to have been destroyed in quantity, but a considerable number do survive in certain local record offices. Hampshire County Record Office, for example, was used as a place of deposit for these forms by the local district valuation office. The forms are of great value as they include the landowners' own descriptions of their property, only part of which was transcribed into the Field Books.

The PRO has examples of Forms 4 relating to Admiralty lands (ADM 116/1279), and lands of the Forestry Commission (F 6/16) and the Rhymney Railway Company (RAIL 1057/1714). The latter include copies of the instructions for completion of the forms - see illustration 12.

Other Records

Some other records held by the PRO may be of interest to family and local historians seeking more background information on the implementation of the survey.

A record of each district valuation office, and the progress of the survey up to the end of 1912, is in IR 74/148. This provides some fascinating detail on the way the survey was carried out, the various types of records created, the staff employed, and the premises where they worked.

An account of the Valuation Office's history and responsibilities was produced in 1920. It is especially useful for the background to the planning and implementation of the survey (IR 74/218).

The calculation of increment value duty is described in IR 83/54.

The record of one famous test case, concerned with the valuation of Model Farm, Norton Malreward, Somerset (Lady Emily Frances Smyth v Commissioners of Inland Revenue), is in IR 40/2502.

ILLUSTRATION 25   INF 3/1744
'The Second World War farm', as seen by an artist working for the Ministry of Information. Note the pylons, telephone lines, tractor, and land girl. The soldier's role in the scene is not clear; perhaps he was there to guard prisoners-of-war working on the land. Original artwork.

5. THE NATIONAL FARM SURVEY, 1941 - 1943

Historical Background

In September 1939, at the beginning of the Second World War, Britain was faced with an urgent need to increase food production. She could no longer depend upon imports of foodstuffs or fertilisers, and it was vital that large areas of land be brought back under cultivation. Under Defence (General) Regulation 49 the Minister of Agriculture and Fisheries was empowered to set up County War Agricultural Executive Committees, similar to those that had been established during the First World War, to which the authority to increase food production was delegated. The powers of the Committees included the directing of different types of cultivation, the organization of labour, the reclamation of derelict land, the inspection of property, and, in extreme cases of bad management, the termination of tenancies and taking possession of land. Much of the day to day work of the Committees was executed by district committees and sub-committees, while the Executive Committee itself maintained a general supervisory role.

One of the first responsibilities of the County War Agricultural Executive Committees was to direct a ploughing-up campaign under which large expanses of grassland (in some areas land that had not seen the plough since medieval, or even prehistoric, times) were prepared for cultivation. To assist in this campaign, in June 1940 a farm survey was initiated with the immediate purpose of increasing food production. Farms were classified in terms of their productive state, A, B, or C, those categories relating more to the physical condition of the farm and its land than the managerial efficiency (or otherwise) of the farmer. Between June 1940 and the early months of 1941 some eighty-five per cent of the agricultural area was surveyed in this manner (all but the smallest farms).

Once the short-term objective of increasing food production had been met, thought was given to implementing a more general National Farm Survey with a longer-term purpose of providing data that would form the basis of post-war agricultural planning. Such a survey had, in fact, been considered in the immediate pre-war years, but had been turned down on the grounds of being too 'Socialist' or 'Germanic'. The National Farm Survey was described at the time as a 'Second Domesday Book', a 'permanent and comprehensive record of the conditions on the farms of England and Wales'. Its ultimate destination, as part of the national archive at the Public Record Office, was anticipated from its inception.

In April 1941 the County War Agricultural Executive Committees received a circular letter from the Ministry of Agriculture and Fisheries setting out the scope and purpose of the more extended survey. This would consist of three components:-

1. A Primary Farm Record for each farm, providing information on conditions of tenure and occupation; and on the natural state of the farm, including its fertility, the adequacy of its equipment, and of its water and electricity supplies, the degree of infestation with weeds or pests, and the management condition of the farm.

2. The complete 4 June 1941 agricultural census return for the farm, including statistics of crop acreages and livestock numbers, and information on rent and length of occupancy.

3. A plan of the farm showing its boundaries and the fields contained in it.

Every farm and agricultural holding of five acres and more was to be surveyed, including those of market gardeners, horticulturists, and poultry-keepers. Holdings of one to five acres, in fact, represented less than one per cent of the total area of crops and grass and were subject to a separate survey of the horticultural sub-committees of the County War Agricultural Executive Committees.

The survey was begun in the spring of 1941, and largely completed by the end of 1943. It was administered by a Farm Survey Supervisory Committee on behalf of the government's Advisory Economists. The County War Agricultural Executive Committees were responsible for the completion of the maps and for the inspection of the farms. The latter was carried out by experienced, practical farmers who visited each farm and interviewed the farmer. Eleven Provincial Agricultural Advisory Centres were responsible for checking the records obtained by the Committees and matching them with the 4 June 1941 census returns that formed the second component of the survey. They also arranged the records and filed them away. Later, the huge task of the statistical analysis of the data obtained was begun, a summary report of which was published in 1946. Some 300,000 farms and other holdings were involved in the survey. The cost was £20,000.

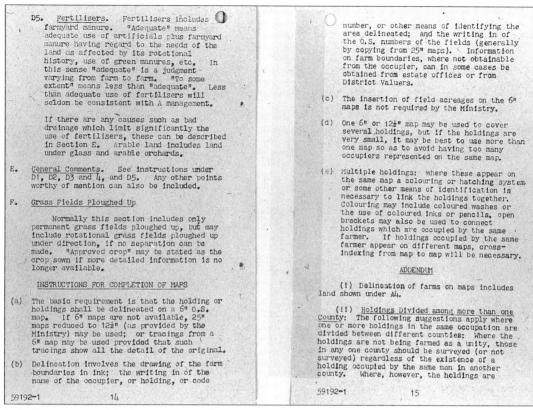

ILLUSTRATION 26   MAF 38/207, f 37
Two pages from the instructions issued in November 1941 to the County War Agricultural Executive Committees for the completion of the primary farm record.

The Records and How to Use Them

The individual farm records of the National Farm Survey, 1941 to 1943, form the record class MAF 32. The maps, which serve also as a graphic index to the farms, make up the class MAF 73.

The Individual Farm Records (MAF 32)

How to Find the Record

The records are arranged by county (the class list includes an index to the counties as they are not arranged alphabetically), and then alphabetically by parish within each county. The code number given to the parish by the survey is also shown in the class list (this is the same system of code numbers as that used for the Parish Summaries of Agricultural Returns (MAF 68) - see page 66).

The MAF 32 Class List

If you know the parish in which the farm whose record you are seeking lies, then you can go straight to the class list for MAF 32. The left-hand column of the relevant page showing that parish contains the piece number you will require. You will then need to add the appropriate parish code number from the list to the piece number to obtain the full reference to order the individual farm records for that parish, eg MAF 32/577/186 (the farm records for the parish of Wennington in Lancashire).

These records will be produced in the main reading room (the Langdale Room), but you can, if required, request that they be sent to the Map Room so that they can be consulted in conjunction with the maps.

This margin not to be used	Reference	Parish No.	County	Parish
		NATIONAL FARM SURVEY (1941)		
		INDIVIDUAL FARM RECORDS		
	(M.A.F. 32)			
			LANCASHIRE (contd.)	
	(577)	324		Wardle
		443		Warrington (C.B.)
		420		Warton
		27		Waterloo
		273		Weeton with Preese
		(186)		Wennington
		238		Westby with Plumptons
		73		Westhoughton
	578	"		"
		123		Whalley
		268		Wheelton

ILLUSTRATION 27
Part of a page from the MAF 32 class list showing Wennington in Lancashire. In this example, the components forming the reference, MAF 32/577/186, have been circled.

If you do not know the parish of your farm (or it is a very large parish and you want to obtain the individual farm number that it was accorded by the survey), then turn to the section beginning on page 63 describing the Maps (MAF 73).

The farm records for each parish are contained loose within large envelopes or folders which are labelled with the parish name and the parish code number (in some cases an additional code number precedes the parish number, that of the Crop Reporter - see below). The various forms used for the separate parts of the survey are grouped together, and each part is arranged by the numerical sequence of farm numbers.

PLEASE DO NOT ALTER the order in which you find the documents: if any appear to be out of order, then inform an officer in the reading room.

The Farm Code References

Each part of the farm record contains the name of the farm and of the farmer and his address, and can, of course, be identified by that information. It also shows the code, unique to that farm, normally in three parts, eg WD 19/37 - firstly, the abbreviation for the county (Westmorland), followed by the parish number (Beetham), and then the individual farm number. Unusually, a fourth part to the reference is given, eg FT 57/7/3 - in this case, the code number, 57, of the Crop Reporter has been added to the reference, which is to farm 3 of parish 7 in Flintshire. If you have used the Maps to identify your farm, it will be this farm code that you will have taken from the map and be seeking on the farm record.

The Content of the Record

The individual farm record is made up of four forms, usually arranged in the following order:-

a. A return of 4 June 1941, showing details of small fruit, vegetables, and stocks of hay and straw. This return was mailed to the farmer, and completed and returned by him.

b. A return of 4 June with respect to agricultural land, providing details of crops and grass, livestock (including horses), and labour employed (returned as above).

c. The Farm Survey - the 'primary survey' that was partly obtained in the field by inspection and interview. The two-sided form is dated twice - when the field information was recorded, and when the record was completed in the office. The Farm Survey is discussed further on pages 58-59.

d.   A further return of 4 June (returned as (a) and (b)), with additional questions on labour, motive power, tractors, rent payable, and length of occupancy. This return was in addition to the usual annual census questions represented by (a) and (b) with which farmers were familiar. The farmers seem to have resented these supplementary questions, and 60,000 first reminders that they must be completed had to be sent out.

The Farm Survey Form

The Primary Record on the Farm Survey form was arranged under six main headings:-

       Tenure
       Conditions of Farm
       Water and Electricity
       Management
       General Comments
       Grass Fields Ploughed Up

Information is provided under these headings on the owner of the farm, if the occupier is a tenant, whether the farmer is full or part time, and whether he occupies other land. The type of soil is indicated, as well as the situation of the farm in relation to roads and railways. The condition of its buildings, drainage, and fences is given, and whether it is infested with rodents or weeds. Details of water and electricity supply are shown. The grass fields (indicated by their Ordnance Survey parcel numbers) ploughed up for the 1940 and 1941 harvests are listed. In the General Comments section, there is sometimes a vivid word picture of the farm and its state of cultivation.

The A, B, C Management Classification

Under the Management heading is perhaps the most controversial part of the survey and the one for which it is often best remembered. It was here that the recorder had to classify the farm as A, B, or C , and, if B or C and due to 'personal failings', he was also obliged to supply additional details.

There was a change in emphasis from the A, B, and C classification of the 1940 survey which had related primarily to the physical condition of the farm. The classification now referred much more to the management condition of the farm, ie how did a farmer manage his resources - well (A); fairly (B); or badly (C)? It was quite possible to have a farmer of A capabilities managing a farm where productivity was low because of poor soils. In which case, his classification would be A, and not B or C.

B or C categories could be given for reasons of old age and lack of capital. If accorded for reasons of personal failings, then these might be amplified as due to (a) physical incapacity brought about by poor health, loss of limbs, or the decease of a farmer leaving his widow to carry on; (b) mental imperfections, such as lack of ambition, stupidity, laziness, and ignorance; and (c) weaknesses of the flesh, such as drunkenness.

Of the 300,000 farms and holdings classified by the survey, fifty-eight per cent were A; thirty-seven per cent B; and five per cent C. The latter figure represents some 15,000 farms.

There is little doubt that this classification system was unevenly applied throughout the country. Some complete parishes, for example, within certain counties, have straight runs of A farms, and others of B. It seems that some inspectors did, in fact, have difficulty distinguishing between a farm, poor on account of its land, and one with genuine bad management.

The information on the management classification was kept strictly confidential. Partly as a result of the need to respect this confidentiality, the National Farm Survey records were closed to public inspection for fifty years, and only became available in 1992.

FARM SURVEY

TOTAL 40 176
ARABLE 20 20
PASTURE 20 20
Code No. NK 53/7

County _Norfolk_
District K _Walsingham_   Parish _Stiffkey_
Name of holding _Old Hall_   Name of farmer _Henry Williamson_
Address of farmer _Coast Road, Stiffkey, Wells_
Number and edition of 6-inch Ordnance Survey Sheet containing farmstead _9 N.W. 1906._

A. TENURE.					
1. Is occupier tenant	...	...	...	...	
owner		...	...	...	X
2. If tenant, name and address of owner :—					
3. Is farmer full time farmer	...	...	...		X
part time farmer	...	...	...		
spare time farmer	...	...	...		
hobby farmer		...	...		
other type	...	...	...		
Other occupation, if any :—					

			Yes	No
4. Does farmer occupy other land ?				X

Name of Holding	County	Parish

			Yes	No
5. Has farmer grazing rights over land not occupied by him ?				X
If so, nature of such rights—				

B. CONDITIONS OF FARM.

1. Proportion (%) of area on which soil is	Heavy	Medium	Light	Peaty
		75	25	

	Yes				
2. Is farm conveniently laid out ?	Yes ...	...			
	Moderately				
	No ...	...			X

	Good	Fair	Bad
3. Proportion (%) of farm which is naturally		40	60
4. Situation in regard to road ...			
5. Situation in regard to railway ...		X	
6. Condition of farmhouse ...			
Condition of buildings ...	...		
7. Condition of farm roads ...	...		
8. Condition of fences ...		X	
9. Condition of ditches ...	...	X	
10. General condition of field drainage		X	
11. Condition of cottages ...			

			No.
12. Number of cottages within farm area	...	...	3
Number of cottages elsewhere ...	...	...	
13. Number of cottages let on service tenancy	...		1

14. Is there infestation with :—			Yes	No
rabbits and moles	...	...		X
rats and mice	...	...		X
rooks and wood pigeons	...			X
other birds	...	...		X
insect pests	...	...		X
15. Is there heavy infestation with weeds ?				X
If so, kinds of weeds :—				

				Yes	No
16. Are there derelict fields ?	...	...			X
If so, acreage	...	...	...		

Form No. B496/E.I.

C. WATER AND ELECTRICITY.

Water supply :—	Pipe	Well	Roof	Stream	None
1. To farmhouse ...		X			
2. To farm buildings ...		X			
3. To fields					X

	Yes	No
4. Is there a seasonal shortage of water ?...		X

Electricity supply :—						
5. Public light	...	...	...	...		X
Public power	...	...	...	...		X
Private light	...	...	...			X
Private power	...	...	...			X
6. Is it used for household purposes ?			...			
Is it used for farm purposes ?	...		...			

D. MANAGEMENT.

1. Is farm classified as A, B or C ?		A

2. Reasons for B or C :—					
old age ...	...	...	...	...	
lack of capital ...	...	...	...		
personal failings	...	...	...		
If personal failings, details :—					

	Good	Fair	Poor	Bad
3. Condition of arable land ...		X		
4. Condition of pasture			X	

	Adequate	To some extent	Not at all
5. Use of fertilisers on :— arable land ...	X		
grass land ...			X

Field information recorded by

C. F. Cass

Date of recording _30/12/41_

This primary record completed by

W. R. Raines

Date _18/2/42_

*15946. Wt.46166/817. 3000 pads. 3/41. Wy.L.P. Gp.676.

ILLUSTRATION 28   MAF 32/739/531

The author, Henry Williamson, farmed in Norfolk from 1937, and throughout the war years. He recounted his struggle to improve the condition of his farm in his book, *The Story of a Norfolk Farm*, published in 1941. The farm and its inspection for the National Farm Survey are also described in his autobiographical novel, *Lucifer Before Sunrise*, published in 1967. He was immensely proud of his A classification accorded by 'the New Domesday scribe'.
The front page (reduced) of the Primary Record for Henry Williamson's farm at Stiffkey. The farm code reference is NK 531/7.

S.F.

MINISTRY OF AGRICULTURE AND FISHERIES
AGRICULTURAL RETURN, 4th JUNE, 1941.

LABOUR ON 4th JUNE (Supplementary Questions).

			Number
129	Of the **REGULAR** workers returned on page I (Questions 73—76) how many are:— WHOLE TIME FAMILY WORKERS { father, mother, son, daughter, brother, sister of } { occupier or his wife, but **not** other relations }	male	
130		female	
131	Of the **CASUAL** workers returned on page I (Questions 77—79) how many are:— EMPLOYED ON THE HOLDING THROUGHOUT THE } YEAR BUT FOR ONLY PART OF THEIR TIME }	male	
132		female	1

MOTIVE POWER ON HOLDING ON 4th JUNE.

	FIXED OR PORTABLE ENGINES (Excluding Motor Tractors)	Number in figures	Horse Power of each
133	Water Wheels or Turbines in present use		
134	Water Wheels not in use, but easily repairable		
135	Steam Engines		
136	Gas Engines		
137	Oil or Petrol Engines		
138	Electric Motors		
139	Others (state kinds)		

	TRACTORS	Number in figures	Horse Power of each	Make or Model of Tractor
140	Wheel Tractors for field work	1	22	*Fordson*
141	Wheel Tractors for stationary work only	1	22	*Austin 23 yrs old*
142	Track laying Tractors			

NOTE.—Subject to the special Question No. 134 engines or tractors that have been discarded or worn out should not be included.

RENT

ANNUAL RENT PAYABLE FOR THE HOLDING TO WHICH THIS RETURN RELATES.

		£
143	State the actual rent payable during the current year (*i.e.*, the contract rent less any abatements but **including** any interest payable on improvements)	
144	If the holding is **owned** by you, give the best estimate you can of the annual rental value	*150*

		Acres	£
145	If the holding is partly owned and partly rented by you, state:— Acreage of land which you own and its estimated rental value **and**		
146	Acreage of land which you hold as tenant and the rent payable (for definition of rent see Question No. 143)		

LENGTH OF OCCUPATION OF HOLDING.

147	How many years have you been the occupier of the holding to which this Return relates ?	*Succeeded my Father*	36	Years *ago*
	or			
148	If you have occupied parts of the holding for different periods, give length of occupation for each {	Part 1..............acres..............years Part 2..............acres..............years Part 3..............acres..............years		

FOR OFFICIAL USE ONLY.

ILLUSTRATION 29   **MAF 32/223/400**
The 4 June 1941 Agricultural Return form containing supplementary questions that were resented by certain farmers. 60,000 reminders to complete this form had to be sent out.

				Yes	No
ay.					
...	...	✗			
...	...	-			
...	...	-			
...	...	-			
...	...	-			

	Yes	No
	-	✗

Parish

	Yes	No
land not	-	✗
... ...		

FARM.

ium	Light	Peaty
)O	-	-
Yes		-
Moderately		-
No		✗

is	Good	Fair	Bad
..	-	50	50
..	✗	·	-
..	-	-	✗
..	✗	-	-
..	-	✗	-
..	-	✗	-
..	-	·	✗
..	-	✗	-
e	✗	·	-
..	✗	-	·

	No.
area ...	1
... ...	-

---

4. Is there a seasonal shortage of water ?...	Yes	No
	✗	-

Electricity supply :—
5. Public light ... ...
Public power ... ...
Private light ... ...
Private power ... ...
6. Is it used for household purposes ? ...
Is it used for farm purposes ? ... ...

D. MANAGEMENT.

1. Is farm classified as A, B or C ? ... ... **C**

2. Reasons for B or C :—
old age ... ...
lack of capital ... ... ✗
personal failings ... ... ✗

If personal failings, details :—

Lack of Capital Initiative
Bad Management.
Supervision needed.

	Good	Fair	Poor	Bad
3. Condition of arable land ...	-	-	✗	-
4. Condition of pasture ...	-	-	✗	-

	Adequate	To some extent	Not at all
5. Use of fertilisers on :— arable land ...	-	✗	-

ILLUSTRATION 30   **MAF 32/223/400**
An example of a 'C' farm in Northumberland and the type of comments recorded by the farm assessor.

The Maps (MAF 73)

Many of the County War Agricultural Executive Committees experienced great difficulties in completing the requirement of the survey to produce a set of plans that showed the boundaries and fields of each farm and holding within their counties. This work was done using the Ordnance Survey 25 inch sheets (reduced to half-size at approximately twelve and a half inches to the mile - 1:5000) or the 6 inch sheets (1:10560). The map sheets themselves were in short supply, the photographic reduction work took a great deal of time, and the transference of the farm areas and boundaries, with their references, to the maps was work of the most exacting nature. Consequently, for many counties, this was the last component of the National Farm Survey to be completed.

The work was done to greatly differing standards. At best, each farm is identified by different colour washes (sometimes a full wash over the whole area of the farm, but often just the boundaries highlighted), and its code reference shown in black ink, together with cross referencing to additional land holdings of the particular farm and the map sheets on which these appear. If 6 inch sheets were used, the survey required that each Ordnance Survey parcel number be taken from a 25 inch sheet and added to the 6 inch sheets in manuscript. This often led to a cluttering of information, with the farm codes in danger of being confused with the Ordnance Survey parcel numbers. To guard against this, the Committee draughtsmen would sometimes use the margins of a 6 inch sheet to show by a series of colour codes the land holdings and their code numbers, whereas the actual surface of the map would be left free for the parcel numbers to be added. However, not all 6 inch map sheets were completed to these high standards.

The Ministry of Agriculture and Fisheries instructed the Committees not to allow the map sheets to be taken into the field: they were meant as record sheets rather than working maps. In some cases, however, it appears that these instructions were ignored, and a number of pencilled notes can be found on certain map sheets. Sometimes the names of farms and of landowners, and their addresses, are added, together with details of land usage, building development and military requisition (eg airfield construction).

How to Find and Use the Maps

Index Grids

1.   If you do not know the name of a farm or its code number, but just the approximate area where it lay (many farms, of course, will have long since disappeared under urban expansion), then **consult first** the volume of index sheets that has the reference, **MAF 73/64**, which is in the central map reference cabinet in the Map Room. This contains in county alphabetical order for England, then Wales, index maps that provide the reference of Ordnance Survey sheets at the 25 inch and 6 inch scales. The index sheets have a grid superimposed upon them that enables this information to be found (as set out in 3. below). The sheets show topographical detail to help you identify the area you require, and they include parish boundaries and names.

2. When you have found the location you are seeking, note the large stamped number added to the index sheet at its right- hand corner. This number forms the second component of the document reference you will need to order your map (the first being that of the class), eg MAF 73/31...(for Northumberland).

3. Next, note the number in the centre of the large grid rectangle in which your area falls, eg 69. This provides the third component, MAF 73/31/69, which is the full reference to order the set of maps relating to that numbered rectangle for Northumberland. The maps are produced in the Map Room.

If the County War Agricultural Executive Committee was using reduced sheets of the 25 inch scale, then there should be sixteen sheets making up the set (each large numbered rectangle is divided by sixteen, as shown on the grid index sheets).

4. When you receive the folder of maps that you have ordered, you will see that the maps are arranged in numerical order, 1-16 (if 25 inch), or from NW to SE (if 6 inch).

PLEASE BE CAREFUL to replace the maps that you have used in this order.

The farm you are seeking will be identified on the map by its code reference, generally the parish and farm number, eg 722/12 (see page 57). Any other lands relating to this farm or holding on adjacent map sheets will normally be indicated as well by the appropriate Ordnance Survey map reference. If two or more holdings are in common ownership, but are being treated by the survey as separate units, then the reference codes of the additional holding/s are often added to the map.

5. When you have obtained the reference code to your farm, you should also have found from the map, or the index sheet, the parish in which it lies. With this information, you can turn next to the MAF 32 class list, and find the piece number containing the farm records for that parish (see page 57). If you cannot find the parish name, you will need to search the MAF 32 class list under the particular county until you find the parish which accords with the parish code number you have obtained from the map.

6. **The MAF 73 Class List** can be used to see the counties set out with their piece numbers and the number-ranges of the Ordnance Survey sheets for each county. The list shows where sheets are 'wanting'. Unfortunately, in certain cases the mapping was never completed, or the maps have been lost before transfer to the PRO. It will also be found that other sheets are 'wanting' from within the large numbered rectangle sets. No maps, of course, were included for urban areas with no agricultural land, and these are the numbers marked 'not used' in the class list. The inside flap of the folders containing the maps is stamped with an index grid showing which maps are included.

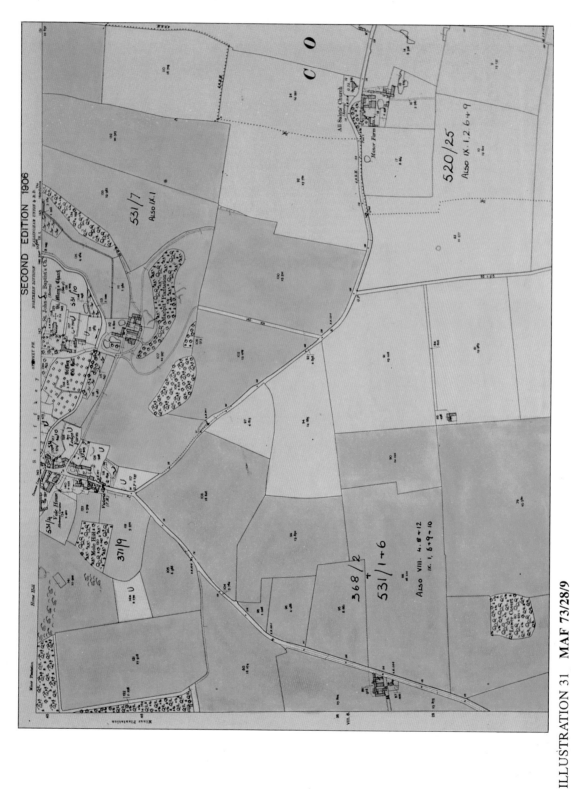

ILLUSTRATION 31 MAF 73/28/9
Part of Ordnance Survey 1:2500 sheet, Norfolk IX.5 (reduced), showing Old Hall Farm, Stiffkey (farm code no 531/7), farmed by Henry Williamson. The annotation, 'also IX.1' means that the area of the farm is continued on that sheet.

Additional Records of the National Farm Survey

Minutes of the County War Agricultural Executive Committees, and of their various sub-committees, some volumes of which have detailed indexes that include farm names, are held in MAF 80. These records have a closure period of fifty years.

Records of the planning and implementation of the two surveys of 1940 and of 1941-1943 are contained within the record class MAF 38. The appropriate sections of the class are: MAF 38/206-217; MAF 38/469-473; and MAF 38/865-867. A copy of the 'Revised Instructions for the Completion of Farm Records and Maps', 1941, is in MAF 38/207. Instructions for the completion of the 4 June 1941 returns are included in MAF 38/470.

Summarized reports by county of the 1940 survey are in MAF 38/213. No individual farm records of the 1940 survey appear to survive. A proof copy of the *National Farm Survey, England & Wales (1941-1943): a Summary Report* (HMSO, 1946), together with copies of press releases, is in MAF 38/216. Statistical analysis of the National Farm Survey arranged by county is in MAF 38/852-863.

Ministry of Agriculture and Fisheries Divisional Office Records (MAF 145- MAF 149 and MAF 157- MAF 182) contain some information on both the 1940 and 1941-1943 surveys. In particular, the Records for Oxfordshire (MAF 168) include individual cases of farms taken into the control of the County War Agricultural Executive Committee, as well as records of the ploughing-up of the Berkshire downlands.

Related Records

MAF 68

Parish Summaries of Agricultural Returns: statistics calculated from the yearly census returns, of which the 4 June 1941 returns in the National Farm Survey provide a unique survival.

MAF 65

Parish Lists for June 1941: arranged by county and parish, sometimes with the Lists for June 1940 attached. These provide the full postal address of each farm within the parish, and of the owner (if not owner/occupier), with statistics of acreages under cultivation. The difference in the area of each holding between 1940 and 1941, and the reason for this, are also given.

These records are currently being prepared at the PRO for public access.

6. RECORDS IN SCOTLAND

This book is concerned principally with the records of the three land surveys as they affect England and Wales. For readers with Scottish interests, a few notes relating to that country are added here. The situation in Ireland is beyond the scope of this book, and readers should make enquiry of the Public Record Office of Northern Ireland, 66 Balmoral Avenue, Belfast BT9 6NY and the National Archives of Ireland, Bishop Street, Dublin 2.

The equivalent of tithes in Scotland were 'teinds'. These were payable by the owners of heritable property within a parish, at first in kind and then by money. The system was never a burden on the land as in England and Wales, and there was no Scottish equivalent of the Tithe Commutation Act 1836 and no resulting land survey. The system of teinds was ended by Act of Parliament in 1925. The Scottish Record Office holds records of the Teind Court and Commissioners in its record classes TE 1-6 (pre-1700), and TE 7-32 (post-1700). Records of teinds are also held amongst private and estate records.

The Finance Act (1909-1910) 1910 made provision as well for a survey and land valuation of Scotland. This was administered by the Valuation Office, which divided Scotland into twelve valuation districts for the purpose. The Scottish Record Office holds the resulting records - Record Maps in the classes IRS 101-133 and Field Books in IRS 51-88.

The National Farm Survey was also extended to Scotland, but in a more limited form than was carried out in England and Wales. The Scottish Record Office holds Farm Boundary Plans (RHP 75001-75285), but no individual farm records. Parish Summaries of Agricultural Returns (agricultural statistics) make up the class AF 40, and there are also records of the Scottish Agricultural Executive Committees. An abridged report on the Scottish farm survey is held by the PRO in MAF 38/217.

All enquiries regarding these Scottish records should be addressed to:

> The Scottish Record Office
> West Register House
> Charlotte Square
> Edinburgh
> EH2 4DF

7. THE CARE OF MAPS

Maps are generally 'large documents' and can be unwieldy and difficult to use. Their large flat surfaces are particularly vulnerable to damage. The following are guidelines for the care of the maps produced to you in the Map Room.

1.   Always use a polyester protective sheet (which will be given to you by repository staff) placed over the map. If the map is bigger than the largest available protective sheet, then place the sheet over the map area you are studying and move it accordingly. Even with the protective sheet in place, do not lean on the map or write notes over it. Tracing may, however, be allowed, with the permission of the officer on duty. When tracing, apply only a light pressure to the paper, and anchor your paper with weights rather than with your hands.

2.   Make sure that you have enough room on your map table to view your map safely. On no account let the map hang over the edge of the table where it may be creased or torn.

3.   Many tithe maps are 'rolled maps', and these can be very large to handle. Seek help from staff, if necessary, in removing (and replacing) the protective sleeves, and in unrolling the map. You should anchor the unrolled map, or the portion of it unrolled, with the document weights that will be found on the map tables. Only unroll as much of a map as you wish to view at one time, and then place a protective sheet over this. Do not try to move the map on the table against the document weights, but remove these first.

4.   All the general reading room rules apply equally in the Map Room. Make sure you use only black graphite pencils, and do not bring pens or any other form of writing implement into the room at all. If you need to work with a laptop computer, inform the repository staff and provision can be made for this. Computers may not, however, be used on the map tables, but on one of the side tables only.

5.   When carrying a flat map to the return point, do so by the edges of the map. Support it as fully as you can with your arms. Do not fold it in any way or allow it to flap about as you carry it. Always seek staff assistance if in any doubt or difficulty.

6.   Any damage which you find on a map produced to you should be reported to the officer on duty. This will be particularly likely in the case of Valuation Office maps where, regrettably, a high percentage are in need of conservation treatment. Do not attempt to handle a map if it is clear that by so doing you will damage it further. Your notification of damage will ensure that the map is brought to the attention of the Conservation Department who will add it to their on-going programme of work on these maps.

Your co-operation in respecting these guidelines and rules is greatly appreciated.

8. FURTHER READING

The following is a select list of books and articles which will be of interest to general readers wishing to increase their knowledge of these three great land surveys.

Tithes

George Brocklehurst, *A Text Book of Tithes and Tithe Rentcharge* (Bale & Co, 1911).

Eric J Evans, *The Contentious Tithe: the Tithe Problem and English Agriculture, 1750-1850* (Routledge & Kegan Paul, 1976).

Roger J P Kain and Hugh C Prince, *The Tithe Surveys of England and Wales* (Cambridge University Press, 1985).

Roger J P Kain and Richard R Oliver, *The Tithe Maps and Apportionments of Mid-Nineteenth Century England and Wales* (Cambridge University Press, 1994).

Michael Sill, 'Using the Tithe Files: a County Durham Study', *The Local Historian*, VII No 4 (November 1986).

Valuation Office

Brian Short, *The Geography of England and Wales in 1910: an Evaluation of Lloyd George's 'Domesday' of Landownership* (Historical Geography Research Series, 1989).

Brian Short and Mick Reed, *Landownership and Society in Edwardian England and Wales: the Finance (1909-10) Act 1910 Records* (University of Sussex, 1987).

Brian Short, Mick Reed, and William Caudwell, 'The County of Sussex in 1910: Sources for a New Analysis', *Sussex Archaeological Collections*, CXXV (1987), 199-224.

Brian Short, 'Local Demographic Studies of Edwardian England and Wales: the Use of the Lloyd George 'Domesday' of Landownership', *Local Population Studies*, LI (Autumn 1993).

The National Farm Survey

P S Barnwell, 'The National Farm Survey 1941-1943', *Journal of the Historic Farm Buildings Group*, VII (1994).

APPENDIX 1

VALUATION OFFICE REGIONS AND DISTRICT OFFICES (WITH PRO CLASS REFERENCES)

Central Region	IR 126	East Anglia Region	IR 127
Aylesbury	1	Basildon	1
Bedfordshire	2	Cambridge	2
East Berkshire	3	Chelmsford	3
Hertfordshire North	4	Colchester	4
Northampton	5	Ipswich	5
Oxford	6	Norwich	6
Reading	7	Peterborough	7
St Albans	8	Peterborough	8
South Buckinghamshire	9	(King's Lynn)	
Watford	10	St Edmundsbury	9

East Midlands Region IR 130		Liverpool Region	IR 132
Boston	1	Chester	1
Derby	2	East Cheshire	2
Grimsby	3	Liverpool	3
Leicester	4	Shropshire	4
Lincoln	5	Stafford	5
Loughborough	6	Stoke-on-Trent	6
Mansfield	7	Warrington	7
Matlock	8	Wigan	8
Nottingham	9		

London Region	**IR 121**		**IR 121**
Merton	1	Harrow (Hillingdon)	12
Barking	2	Hounslow	13
Barnet	3	Islington	14
Bexley & Greenwich	4	Kensington & Chelsea	15
Bromley	5	Lambeth	16
Camden	6	Redbridge	17
City of London	7	Richmond-upon-Thames	18
Croydon	8	Southwark	19
Ealing	9	Tower Hamlets	20
Enfield	10	Westminster 1	21
Hammersmith & Fulham	11	Westminster 2	22

Manchester Region	**IR 133**	**Northern Region**	**IR 135**
Bolton	1	Carlisle	1
East Lancashire	2	Cleveland	2
Lancaster	3	Darlington	3
Manchester	4	Durham	4
Preston	6	Newcastle	5
Rochdale	6	Newcastle (Tyneside)	6
Salford	7	Northumberland	7
Stockport	8	South Lakeland	8
		Sunderland	9

South Eastern Region	**IR 124**	**Western Region**	**IR 131**
Brighton	1	Abergavenny	1
Canterbury	2	Bangor	2
Canterbury (Maidstone)	3	Bangor (Colwyn Bay)	3
Eastbourne	4	Cardiff	4
East Kent	5	Dyfed	5
Medway	6	Merthyr Tydfil	6
Reigate	7	Newport	7
Tunbridge Wells	8	Pontypridd	8
Worthing	9	Swansea	9
		Wrexham	10
		Wrexham (Welshpool)	11

71

Wessex Region	IR 125	**Western Region**	IR 128
Bournemouth	1	Barnstaple	1
Dorset County West	2	Bath	2
Guildford	3	Bristol	3
N E Hampshire	4	Cheltenham	4
North Surrey	5	Cornwall	5
Portsmouth (records destroyed in Second World War)	6	Exeter	6
Salisbury	7	Gloucester	7
Solent	8	Plymouth	8
Solent (IOW)	9	Somerset	9
Southampton (records destroyed in Second World War)	10	Torbay	10
Wiltshire North	11		

West Midlands Region	IR 129	**Yorkshire Region**	IR 134
Birmingham	1	Bradford	1
Coventry	2	Calderdale	2
Hereford & Worcester	3	Doncaster	3
Kidderminster	4	Harrogate	4
Lichfield	5	Hull	5
Sandwell	6	Kirklees	6
Walsall	7	Leeds	7
Warwick	8	Sheffield	8
Wolverhampton	9	Wakefield	9
		York	10

APPENDIX 2

VALUATION OFFICE MAPS

INDEX OF COUNTIES

COUNTY	SCALE	REFERENCE
Anglesey	1:2500/1250/500	IR 131/2
Bedfordshire	1:2500/1250	IR 126/2
	1:2500	IR 127/7
Berkshire	1:2500	IR 126/3
	1:2500	IR 126/6
	1:2500/1250	IR 126/7
Brecknockshire	1:2500/1250	IR 131/1
	1:2500/1250	IR 131/6
	1:2500/1250	IR 131/8
Buckinghamshire	1:2500/1250/500	IR 126/1
	1:2500	IR 126/2
	1:2500/1250	IR 126/3
	1:2500/1250	IR 126/9
Cambridgeshire	1:2500/1250	IR 127/2
	1:2500/1250	IR 127/7
	1:1250	IR 127/9
Cardiganshire	1:2500/1250/500	IR 131/5
Carmarthenshire	1:2500/1250/500	IR 131/5
	1:2500/1250	IR 131/9
Caernarfonshire	1:2500/1250/500	IR 131/2
	1:2500/1250/10560	IR 131/3
Cheshire	1:2500	IR 132/1
	1:2500/1250/528/500	IR 132/2
	1:2500/1250	IR 132/7
	1:2500/1250	IR 133/7
	1:2500/10560	IR 133/8

COUNTY	SCALE	REFERENCE
Cornwall	1:2500	IR 128/5
Cumberland	1:2500/1250/10560	IR 135/1
	1:2500/1250/500	IR 135/8
Denbighshire	1:2500/1250/10560	IR 131/3
	1:2500/1250	IR 131/10
Derbyshire	1:2500/1250/500	IR 130/2
	1:2500/1250	IR 130/8
	1:2500	IR 134/3
	1:2500/1250	IR 134/8
Devon	1:2500/1250/500	IR 128/1
	1:2500	IR 128/5
	1:2500/1250/500	IR 128/6
	1:2500/1250/500	IR 128/8
	1:2500	IR 128/9
	1:2500/1250/500	IR 128/10
Dorset	1:2500/1250	IR 125/1
	1:2500/1250	IR 125/2
Durham	1:2500/1250/500	IR 135/2
	1:2500/1250/10560	IR 135/3
	1:2500/1250/10560	IR 135/4
	1:2500/500	IR 135/5
	1:2500/1250/500	IR 135/9
Essex	1:2500/1250	IR 121/2
	1:2500/1250	IR 121/17
	1:2500	IR 121/20
	1:2500/1250	IR 127/1
	1:2500/1250	IR 127/3
	1:2500/1250	IR 127/4
Flintshire	1:2500/1250	IR 131/10

COUNTY	SCALE	REFERENCE
Glamorganshire	1:2500/1250/500	IR 131/4
	1:2500/1250	IR 131/6
	1:2500/1250	IR 131/8
	1:2500/1250	IR 131/9
Hampshire	1:2500/1250	IR 125/1
	1:2500/1250	IR 125/4
	1:2500	IR 125/7
	1:2500	IR 125/8
	1:2500/10560	IR 125/9
Hampshire (Portsmouth)	RECORDS DESTROYED	IR 125/6
Hampshire (Southampton)	RECORDS DESTROYED	IR 125/10
Herefordshire	1:2500/1250/500	IR 129/3
Hertfordshire	1:2500/1250	IR 121/3
	1:2500	IR 126/2
	1:2500	IR 126/4
	1:2500/1250	IR 126/8
	1:2500/1250	IR 126/10
Huntingdonshire	1:2500/1250	IR 127/7
Kent	1:2500	IR 121/4
	1:2500	IR 121/5
	1:2500/1250	IR 124/2
	1:2500/1250	IR 124/3
	1:2500/1250	IR 124/5
	1:2500	IR 124/6
	1:2500/1250	IR 124/8
Lancashire	1:2500/1250/500	IR 132/3
	1:2500/1250	IR 132/7
	1:2500/1250	IR 132/8
	1:2500/1250	IR 133/1
	1:2500/1250	IR 133/2
	1:2500/1250	IR 133/3

COUNTY	SCALE	REFERENCE
Lancashire (continued)	1:2500/1250/500	IR 133/4
	1:2500/1250/500	IR 133/5
	1:2500/1250/500	IR 133/6
	1:2500/1250/10560	IR 133/8
Leicestershire	1:2500/1250/500	IR 130/4
	1:2500/1250/528/500	IR 130/6
Lincolnshire	1:2500/1250/500	IR 130/1
	1:2500/1250/500	IR 130/3
	1:2500/1250/500	IR 130/5
	1:2500/1250	IR 134/5
London	1:1056	IR 121/1
	1:1056	IR 121/3
	1:1056	IR 121/4
	1:1056	IR 121/5
	1:1056	IR 121/6
	1:1056	IR 121/7
	1:1056	IR 121/9
	1:1056	IR 121/10
	1:1056	IR 121/11
	1:1056	IR 121/13
	1:1056	IR 121/14
	1:1056	IR 121/15
	1:1056	IR 121/16
	1:1250	IR 121/17
	1:1056	IR 121/18
	1:1056	IR 121/19
	1:1250/1056	IR 121/20
	1:1056	IR 121/21
	1:1056	IR 121/22
Merionethshire	1:2500/1250	IR 131/2
	1:2500/1250	IR 131/10
Middlesex	1:2500	IR 121/3
	1:2500	IR 121/9
	1:2500/1250	IR 121/10
	1:2500	IR 121/11

COUNTY	SCALE	REFERENCE
Middlesex (continued)	1:2500	IR 121/12
	1:2500	IR 121/13
	1:2500	IR 121/18
	1:2500	IR 126/10
Monmouthshire	1:2500/1250	IR 131/1
	1:2500	IR 131/4
	1:2500/1250	IR 131/6
	1:2500	IR 131/7
Montgomery	1:2500	IR 131/11
Norfolk	1:2500/1250	IR 127/6
	1:2500/1250/500	IR 127/8
	1:2500/500	IR 127/9
Northamptonshire	1:2500/1250	IR 126/5
	1:2500/1250	IR 127/7
Northumberland	1:2500/500	IR 135/5
	1:2500/500	IR 135/6
	1:2500/1250/528/500/10560	IR 135/7
	1:500	IR 135/9
Nottinghamshire	1:2500/1250	IR 130/7
	1:2500/1250/500	IR 130/9
	1:2500	IR 134/3
Oxfordshire	1:2500	IR 126/1
	1:2500/1250/500	IR 126/6
Pembrokeshire	1:2500/1250	IR 131/5
Radnorshire	1:2500/1250	IR 131/1
Rutland	1:2500/1250	IR 130/6
Shropshire	1:2500/1250/500	IR 132/4

COUNTY	SCALE	REFERENCE
Somerset	1:2500/1250	IR 128/1
	1:2500/1250	IR 128/2
	1:2500/1250	IR 128/3
	1:2500/1250/500	IR 128/9
Staffordshire	1:1250	IR 129/1
	1:2500/1250	IR 129/4
	1:2500/1250	IR 129/5
	1:2500/1250/500	IR 129/6
	1:2500/1250/500	IR 129/7
	1:2500/1250	IR 129/9
	1:2500/1250	IR 132/5
	1:2500/1250	IR 132/6
Suffolk	1:2500/1250/500	IR 127/5
	1:2500	IR 127/6
	1:2500/1250/500	IR 127/9
Surrey	1:2500/1250	IR 121/1
	1:2500	IR 121/8
	1:2500/1250	IR 121/18
	1:2500/1250	IR 124/7
	1:2500/1250	IR 125/3
	1:2500/1250	IR 125/5
Sussex	1:2500/1250/500	IR 124/1
	1:2500	IR 124/4
	1:2500	IR 124/8
	1:2500/1250	IR 124/9
Warwickshire	1:1250/500	IR 129/1
	1:2500/1250	IR 129/2
	1:2500	IR 129/5
	1:2500	IR 129/6
	1:2500	IR 129/7
	1:2500/1250/500	IR 129/8
Westmorland	1:2500/1250/10560	IR 135/1
	1:2500/1250	IR 135/8

COUNTY	SCALE	REFERENCE
Wiltshire	1:2500/1250/500	IR 125/7
	1:2500/1250/500	IR 125/11
	1:2500	IR 128/2
Worcestershire	1:1250/500	IR 129/1
	1:2500/1250/500	IR 129/3
	1:2500/1250/500	IR 129/4
	1:1250/500	IR 129/6
Yorkshire (East Riding)	1:2500/1250/500	IR 134/5
	1:2500	IR 134/10
Yorkshire (North Riding)	1:2500/1250/500	IR 134/4
	1:2500/1250/500/10560	IR 134/10
	1:2500/1250/500	IR 135/2
	1:2500	IR 135/3
	1:10560	IR 135/8
Yorkshire (West Riding)	1:2500/1250/10560	IR 133/2
	1:2500/1250/500/10560	IR 134/1
	1:2500/1250/500/10560	IR 134/2
	1:2500/1250/500	IR 134/3
	1:2500/1250/500	IR 134/4
	1:2500/500	IR 134/5
	1:2500/1250/500	IR 134/6
	1:2500/1250/500	IR 134/7
	1:2500/1250/500	IR 134/8
	1:2500/1250/500	IR 134/9
	1:2500/500	IR 134/10
	1:2500/1250/10560	IR 135/8

APPENDIX 3

VALUATION OFFICE MAPS

INDEX OF PLACES

PLACE	REFERENCE	PLACE	REFERENCE
Abergavenny	IR 131/1	Chester	IR 132/1
Anglesey	IR 131/2	Cleckheaton	IR 134/6
Ashby de la Zouch	IR 130/6	Colchester	IR 127/4
Aylesbury	IR 126/1	Colwyn Bay	IR 131/3
		Congleton	IR 132/2
Bangor	IR 131/2	Coventry	IR 129/2
Barking	IR 121/2	Crewe	IR 132/2
Barnet	IR 121/3	Crewkerne	IR 128/9
Barnsley	IR 134/9	Croydon	IR 121/8
Barnstaple	IR 128/1	Darlington	IR 135/3
Basildon	IR 127/1	Derby	IR 130/2
Bath	IR 128/2	Dewsbury	IR 134/6
Batley	IR 134/6	Doncaster	IR 134/3
Beverley	IR 134/5	Driffield, Great	IR 134/5
Bexley	IR 121/4	Dudley	IR 129/4
Bingley	IR 134/1	Durham	IR 135/5
Birmingham	IR 129/1		IR 135/3
Birstal	IR 134/6		IR 135/4
Bolton	IR 133/1		IR 135/2
Boston	IR 130/1		
Bournemouth	IR 125/1		
Bradford	IR 134/1	Ealing	IR 121/9
Bradford on Avon	IR 125/7	Eastbourne	IR 124/4
Bridgwater	IR 128/9	Elland	IR 134/2
Bridlington	IR 134/5	Ely, Isle of	IR 127/7
Brighouse	IR 134/2	Enfield	IR 121/10
Brighton	IR 124/1	Exeter	IR 128/6
Bristol	IR 128/3		
Bromley	IR 121/5	Farsley	IR 134/1
Bromsgrove	IR 129/4		IR 134/7
Burton on Trent	IR 129/5	Frome	IR 128/9
		Fulham	IR 121/11
Calderdale	IR 134/2		
Cambridge	IR 127/2	Gainsborough	IR 130/5
Camden	IR 121/6	Garston	IR 132/3
Canterbury	IR 124/2	Gateshead	IR 135/9
Cardiff	IR 131/4		IR 135/6
Carlisle	IR 135/1	Glamorgan	IR 131/4
Castleford	IR 134/9	Gloucester	IR 128/7
Chelmsford	IR 127/3	Goole	IR 134/5
Chelsea	IR 121/15	Greenwich	IR 121/4
Cheltenham	IR 128/4	Grimsby	IR 130/3
		Guildford	IR 125/3

PLACE	REFERENCE	PLACE	REFERENCE
Halifax	IR 134/2	Newcastle upon Tyne	IR 135/5
Hammersmith	IR 121/11		IR 135/9
Harrogate	IR 134/4		IR 135/6
Harrow	IR 121/12	Newport (Gwent)	IR 131/7
Hebden Bridge	IR 134/2	Northampton	IR 126/5
Heckmondwike	IR 134/6	Norwich	IR 127/6
Hereford	IR 129/3	Nottingham	IR 130/9
Heywood	IR 133/6		
Hounslow	IR 121/13	Oldham	IR 133/6
Huddersfield	IR 134/6	Oswestry	IR 132/4
Hull	IR 134/5	Otley	IR 134/7
			IR 134/4
Idle	IR 134/1	Oxford	IR 126/6
Ilkley	IR 134/1		
Ipswich	IR 127/5	Peterborough	IR 127/7
Islington	IR 121/14	Plymouth	IR 128/8
		Pontefract	IR 134/9
Jarrow	IR 135/5	Pontypridd	IR 131/8
		Preston	IR 133/5
Keighley	IR 134/1	Pudsey	IR 134/1
Kensington	IR 121/15		IR 134/7
Kidderminster	IR 129/4		
King's Lynn	IR 127/8	Ravensthorpe	IR 134/6
Kingston upon Hull	IR 134/5	Reading	IR 126/7
Kirklees	IR 134/6	Redbridge	IR 121/17
Knottingley	IR 134/9	Reigate	IR 121/17
		Richmond	IR 134/4
Lambeth	IR 121/16	Richmond upon Thames	IR 121/18
Lancaster	IR 133/3	Rochdale	IR 133/6
Leamington Spa	IR 129/8	Rotherham	IR 134/3
Leeds	IR 134/7		IR 134/8
Leicester	IR 130/4	Royton	IR 133/6
Lichfield	IR 129/5		
Lincoln	IR 130/5	Salford	IR 133/7
Lindsey	IR 134/5		IR 133/4
Liverpool	IR 132/3	Salisbury	IR 125/7
London (City of)	IR 121/7	Saltaire	IR 134/1
Loughborough	IR 130/6	Sandwell	IR 129/6
Ludlow	IR 132/4	Sheffield	IR 134/8
		Shepton Mallet	IR 128/9
Maidstone	IR 124/3	Shields (North & South)	IR 135/5
Manchester	IR 133/4	Shipley	IR 134/1
Mansfield	IR 130/7	Shrewsbury	IR 132/4
Matlock	IR 130/8	Skipton	IR 134/4
Medway, The	IR 124/6	Southport	IR IR 132/3
Merthyr Tydfil	IR 131/6	Southwark	IR 121/19
Merton	IR 121/1	Sowerby Bridge	IR 134/2
Middlesbrough	IR 135/2	St Albans	IR 126/8
Middleton	IR 133/6	St Edmundsbury	IR 127/9
Mirfield	IR 134/6		

PLACE	REFERENCE
Stafford	IR 132/5
Stanningley	IR 132/5
	IR 132/5
Stockport	IR 133/8
Stockton-on-Tees	IR 135/2
Stoke-on-Trent	IR 132/6
Stourbridge	IR 129/4
Stratford-on-Avon	IR 129/8
Sutherland	IR 135/9
Swansea	IR 131/9
Taunton	IR 128/9
Todmorden	IR 134/2
Tower Hamlets	IR 121/20
Trowbridge	IR 125/7
Tunbridge Wells	IR 124/8
Tynemouth	IR 135/5
Wakefield	IR 134/9
Wallsend	IR 135/5
Walsall	IR 129/7
Warminster	IR 125/7
Warrington	IR 132/7
Warwick	IR 132/7
Wellington	IR 128/9
Welshpool	IR 131/11
Westminster	IR 121/22
	IR 121/21
Whitehaven	IR 135/8
Wigan	IR 132/8
Wight, Isle of	IR 125/9
Withington	IR 133/4
Wolverhampton	IR 129/9
Worcester	IR 129/3
Worthing	IR 124/9
Wrexham	IR 131/10
Yeovil	IR 128/9
York	IR 134/10

INDEX

A

Addresses
  Farms   57, 63, 66
  Landowners   50, 63
  Property   41
Agricultural census returns   54, 57-58, 61,
  66 *see also* Parish summaries of
  Agricultural Returns
Airfield construction   63
Assessable Site Value   44, 50
Assessment numbers *see* Hereditaments

B

Bakehouses   16
Banks   41
Bomb Census maps   3
Boundary Awards   19
Buildings
  Development   63
  Government buildings   2
  Historic buildings   41
  Maps and plans   2, 25, 35, 41, 46, 50
  Public buildings   41, 49
  Value   44
  see also Property; *and under specific
  types of building*

C

Cathedrals   41
Chancel repairs   19
Churches   19, 41, 46, 49
Coastguard stations   2
Commons   15
  Rights of common   44
Cottages   16, 17
County Diagrams   9, 27
County Record Offices *see* Local record
  offices
County War Agricultural Executive
  Committees   53-55, 63, 64, 66, 67
Crop Reporter numbers   57
Crops *see* Farms

D

District Valuation Offices   22, 25, 26, 30,
  31, 34, 36, 50, 51, 70-72
'Domesday Books' *see* Valuation Books
Drainage   21, 58

E

Estates   44, 51

F

Factories   41
Farm Maps   54, 55, 63-64, 66
Farm Records   55-59, 66
Farm Survey Supervisory Committee   54
Farmers   4, 6, 54
  Addresses   57
  Managerial efficiency   53, 58, 59
  Names   57
Farms
  Addresses   57, 63, 66
  Boundaries   63, 67
  Buildings   58
  Classification   53, 58-60, 62
  Crop acreages   54, 66
  Crop prices   15
  Crop returns   57
  Descriptions   4, 25, 41, 47, 58
  Drainage   58
  Electricity supply   54, 58
  Equipment   54
  Fences   58
  Fertility   54
  Fields   63
  Inspections   54, 60
  Labour employed   57, 58
  Livestock numbers   54, 57
  Management condition   54, 58, 59
  Names   16, 57, 63, 66
  Natural state   54
  Occupancy, length of   54, 58
  Pest infestation   54, 58
  Physical condition   53, 58
  Plans   54
  Rent   54, 58
  Second World War farm   52
  Soil type   58